AF597894

LILY STOCKMAN

MINOTAUR

MASSIMODECARLO IN COLLABORATION WITH
FONDATION LE CORBUSIER

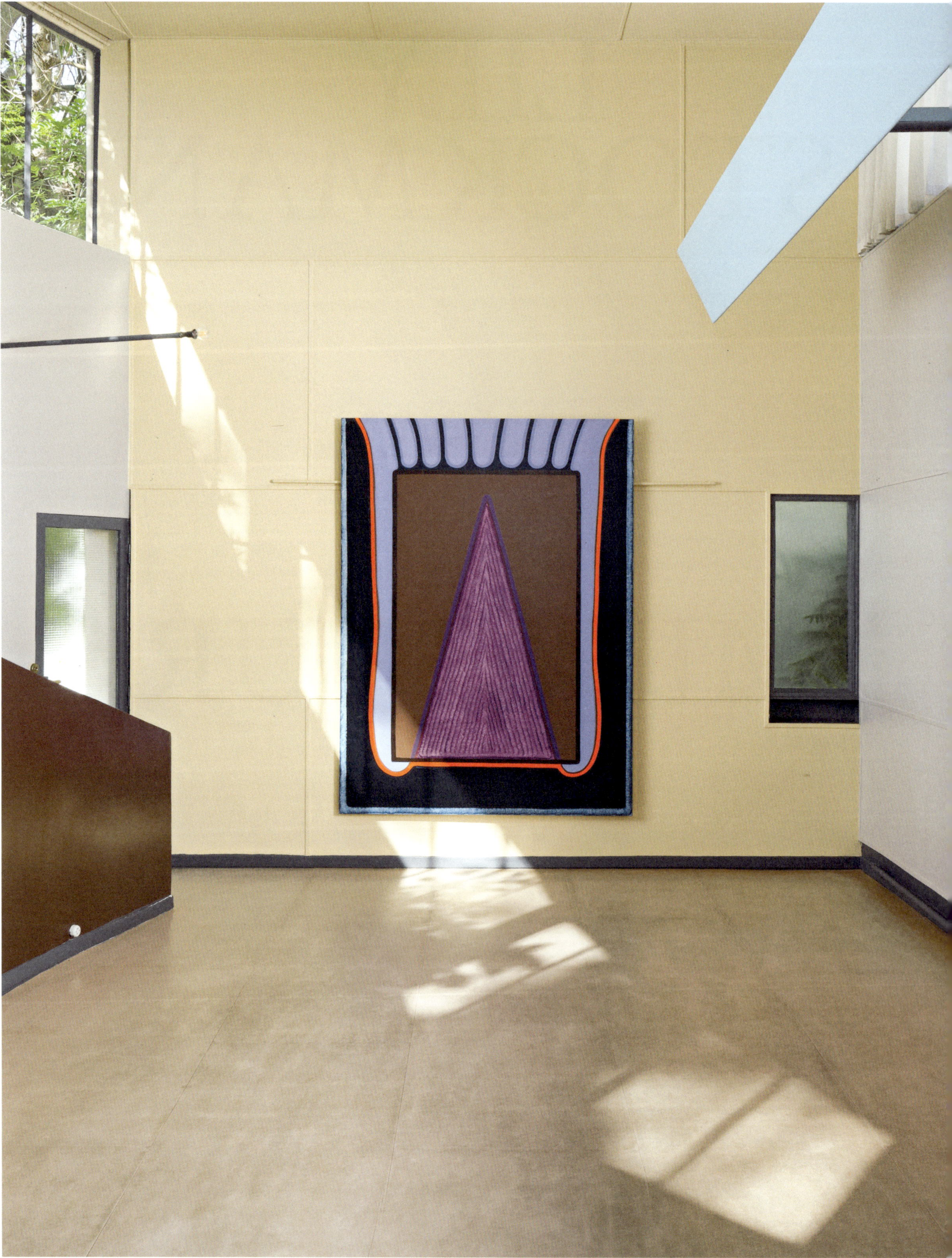

INTRODUCTION
Lily Stockman

In June, 2024, I installed eleven new paintings at Maison La Roche, the house Le Corbusier built for a Swiss art collector in Paris's stately sixteenth arrondissement in 1923–1925. The next-door Maison Jeanneret, is home to Fondation Le Corbusier, the entire archive and braintrust of Corbu's astonishing output, and a UNESCO World Heritage Site. What could I add to this space a century after it was built? If Maison La Roche was the chapel to Corbusier's *Purism* movement, I could make the metaphorical stained glass windows to filter the light of the present tense into the nave of the past.

I spent my undergraduate years studying painting in the Carpenter Center at Harvard, completed in 1963 and Le Corbusier's only building in the United States (hard to believe but true). The painting classes were held in the massive third floor atelier with curved cast concrete walls, supporting pilotis, and yellow window louvers we could open and close to control the clear northern light coming through the hundreds of slender windows. I spent my senior thesis in the top floor studio, the walls of which were almost entirely glass, so that in a blizzard the impression was of being inside a snow globe. Each space in the Carpenter had a distinct relationship with light, volume, and view, and I learned how to compose space and deploy color within the picture plane of Corbusier's physical architectural space. The frames within frames in my work very much come from the glass walls, concrete buttresses, and dislocated volumes of that building.

No matter where we were in the building (save for the subterranean Harvard Film Archive, which was, in a Puritanical flourish, buried underground) we could see the weather, the time of day, and the condition of the season. In spring the redbud trees bloomed pink against their black bark, in fall the locusts and sugar maples exploded into yellow and gold. Winter was bleak in Cambridge, and the building was freezing. We sledded down the signature Corbu ramp when it iced over, and sunbathed on the triangular roof overhang when it was sunny. My paintings reflected all of it. Le Corbusier taught me how to bring the outside inside.

Years later, while I was living in Jaipur and studying Indian miniature painting before attending graduate school, I took a bus eight hours to make a somewhat poorly-planned pilgrimage to Chandigarh to see my old friend Le Corbusier again. The government buildings he designed in the 1950s were being restored at the time and visitors were strictly forbidden, so I spent an afternoon wandering the perimeter of the Capitol Complex and sneaking photographs. The asymmetry of my experience outside his massive, inaccessible government campus in Punjab marked a very different relationship to his architecture—now I was simply a foreigner in proximity to the formal workplace of democracy in a post-Partition capital. I could only encounter this Corbu from a remove.

President Obama was visiting India that weekend and All India Radio was being broadcast from every shop. I bought rose water from a vendor outside in the long shadows of the Palace of Assembly, which Corbu had designed to cast great pleats of shade around the building to keep city workers cool. I thought back to a spring afternoon sitting in the shade under the cantilevered Carpenter, where I encountered my now-husband. I was sitting and sketching, half in light, half in shade, trying to find the right temperature, which he remarked on. Making a painting is the same sort of thing, really—pushing and pulling to find the right balance until something marvelous happens.

Now, nearly twenty years after Cambridge and ten after Chandigarh, I arrive in Paris. Maison La Roche is everything the Carpenter Center and Capitol Complex are not: small, colorful, jaunty, and modest in scale. That mauve dining room, the Paris green and charron blue walls, the workaday black floor tiles and original light fixtures from the hardware store, Le Corbusier, Pierre Jeanneret, and Charlotte Perriand's furniture (a "house" for your resting body), and the bachelor-pad proportions of the house provide the most idiosyncratic and charming of all Corbu's so-called machines for living.

The formal elements of my paintings echo his arabesque ramp, his interplay between open and closed-off space, the invitation to pass from one room into another. In the dappled morning light, the paintings appear like elements of the house. As the light shifts, they camouflage into the space one moment, then open portals into imaginary rooms, or disappear altogether. Half in light, half in shade. In keeping with the Corbusier tradition of keeping records for everything, this book is an artifact of our project.

Lily Stockman
Los Angeles
November 2024

FONDATION LE CORBUSIER AT MAISON LA ROCHE
History and Inspiration

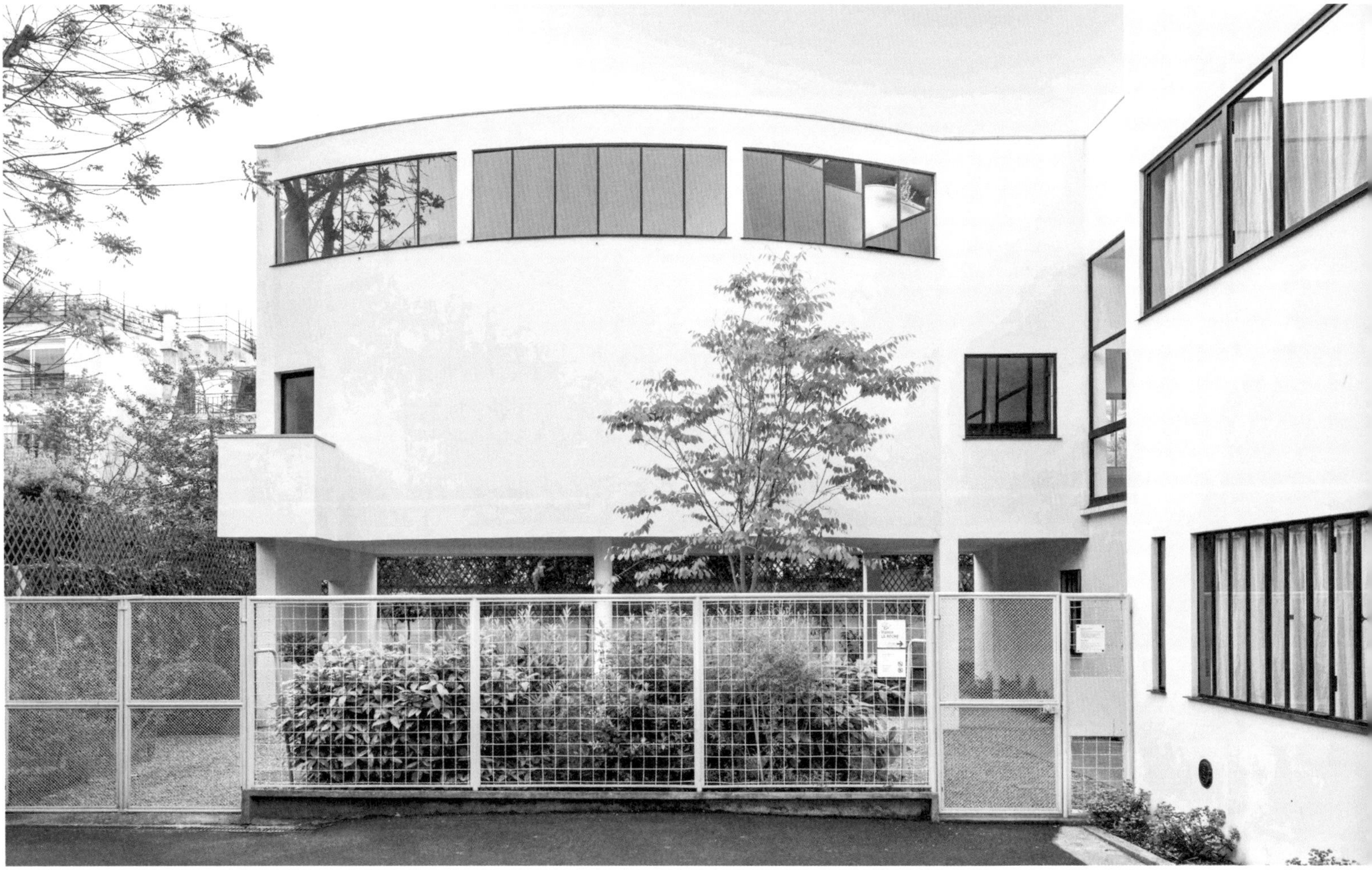

South-eastern facade of Maison La Roche, 2016. © FLC / ADAGP / Olivier Martin-Gambier

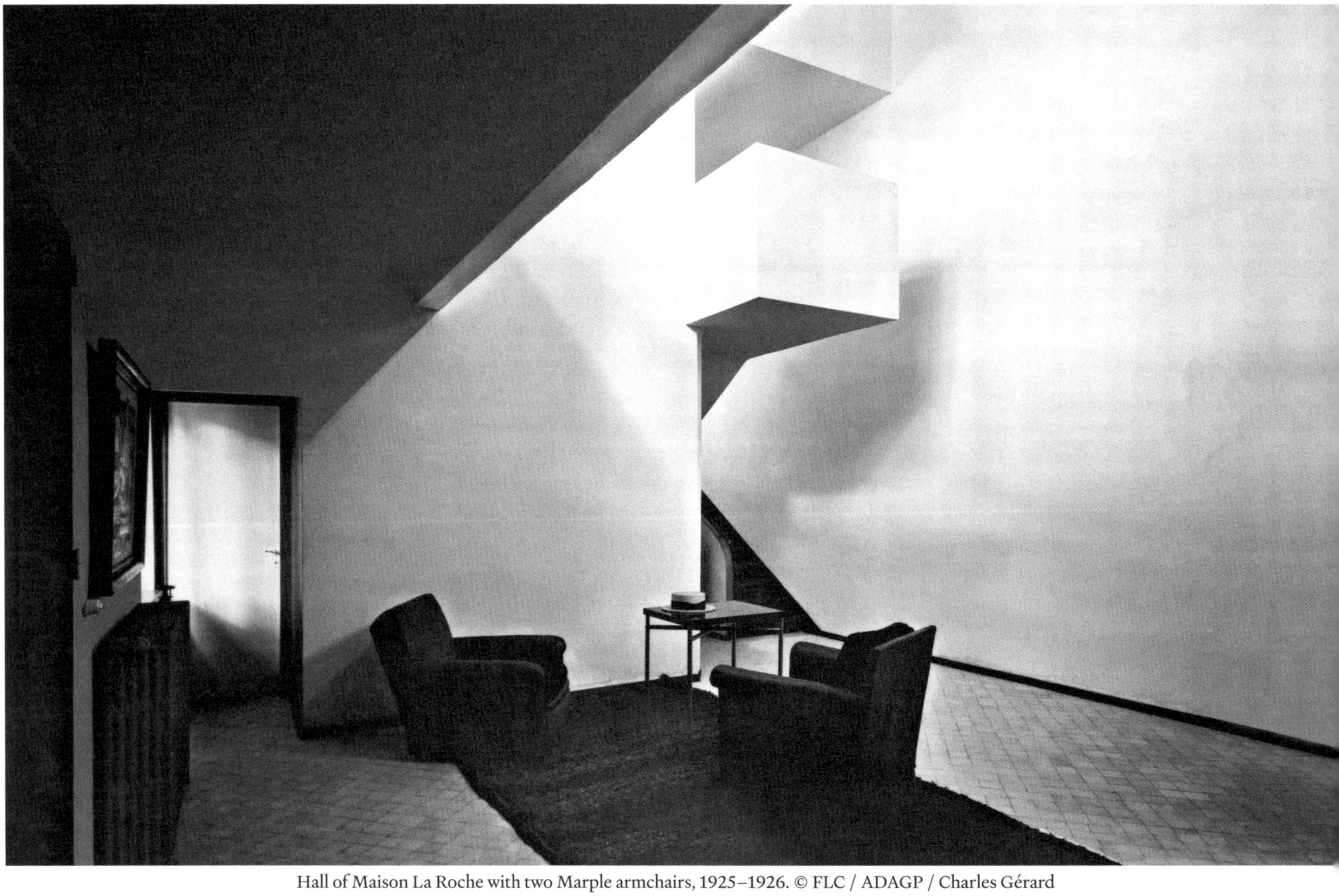

Hall of Maison La Roche with two Marple armchairs, 1925–1926. © FLC / ADAGP / Charles Gérard

Maison La Roche

Designed and built between 1923 and 1925 by Le Corbusier and Pierre Jeanneret, Maison La Roche is widely admired and helped establish Le Corbusier as a master of modernity in architecture. The use of new construction materials allowed him to implement, for the first time, what he would call in 1927 the "five points of a new architecture": the free facade, the free floor plan, long windows, the roof garden, and stilts. According to the wishes of its original owner, Raoul La Roche, a banker and collector of modern art, the house is divided into two parts: the gallery, which presented La Roche's collection of paintings, and his private apartments. Maisons La Roche and Jeanneret have been the subjects of several restoration campaigns since the 1970s. They were classified as Historic Monuments in 1996 and, since 2016, have been (along with sixteen other works by Le Corbusier) on the UNESCO World Heritage List.

Fondation Le Corbusier

Le Corbusier was keen to safeguard his life's work and legacy. Given that he had no direct heir, starting in 1949 he began organizing the creation of a foundation, which was officially inaugurated in 1968, three years after his death. Fondation Le Corbusier is based in Maison Jeanneret, which he built for his brother Albert and his family. The foundation oversees the majority of Le Corbusier's estate, including original drawings, studies, and plans as well as an important collection of written and photographic archives. The more than four hundred thousand items include thirty-five thousand plans, eight thousand drawings, fifteen thousand photographs, and great numbers of paintings, sculptures, engravings, and tapestries. The foundation's mission is the conservation and promotion of Le Corbusier's life's work, embodied by four buildings: Le Corbusier's studio-apartment in Paris, where he lived and worked for almost thirty years; La Petite maison au bord du lac Léman, built for his parents in Corseaux, Switzerland; Maison La Roche, home to his collector friend Raoul La Roche; and Maison Jeanneret.

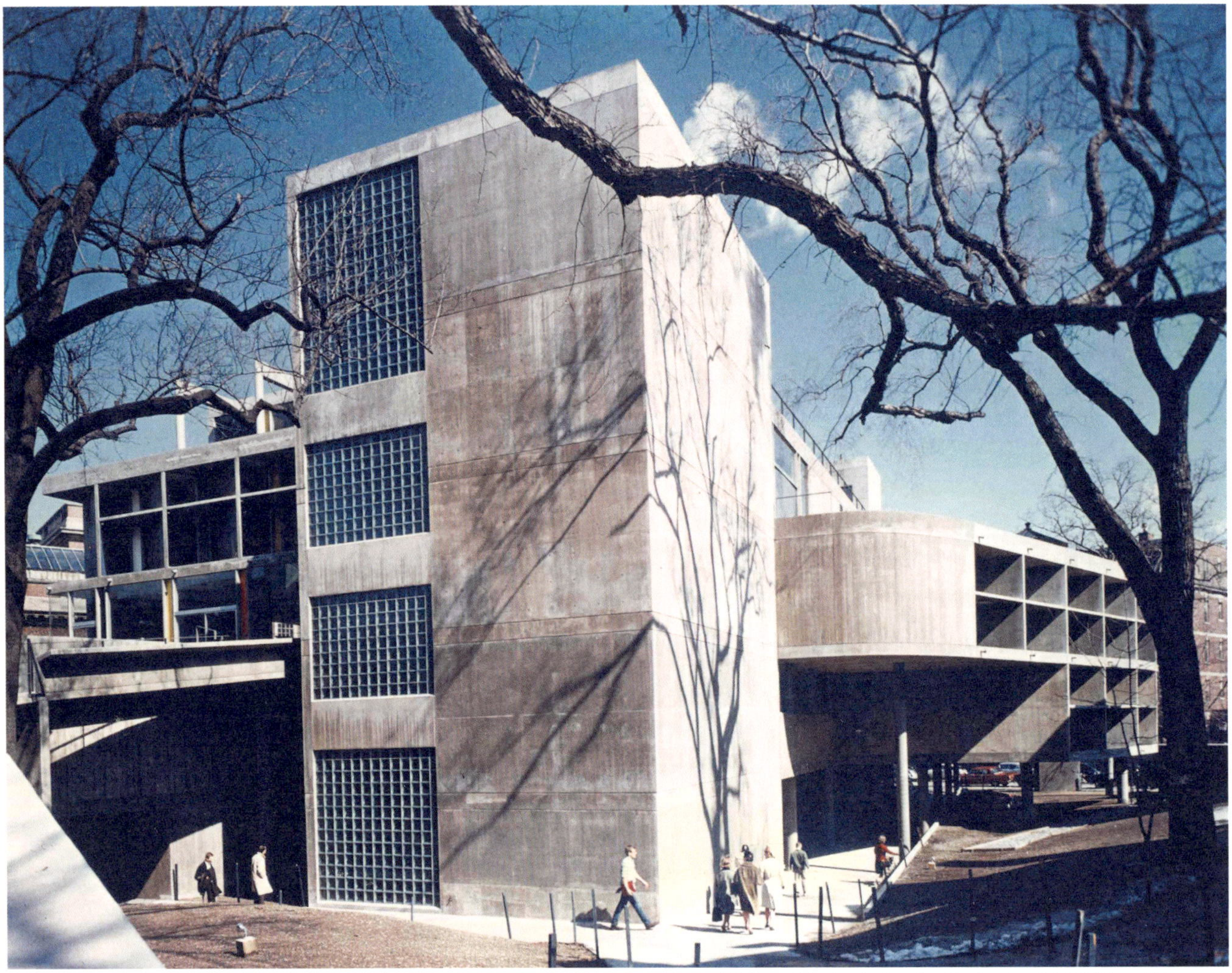

LE CORBUSIER, Carpenter Center for Visual Arts, Cambridge, Etats-Unis, 1959–1961. Fondation Le Corbusier ©FLC/ADAGP

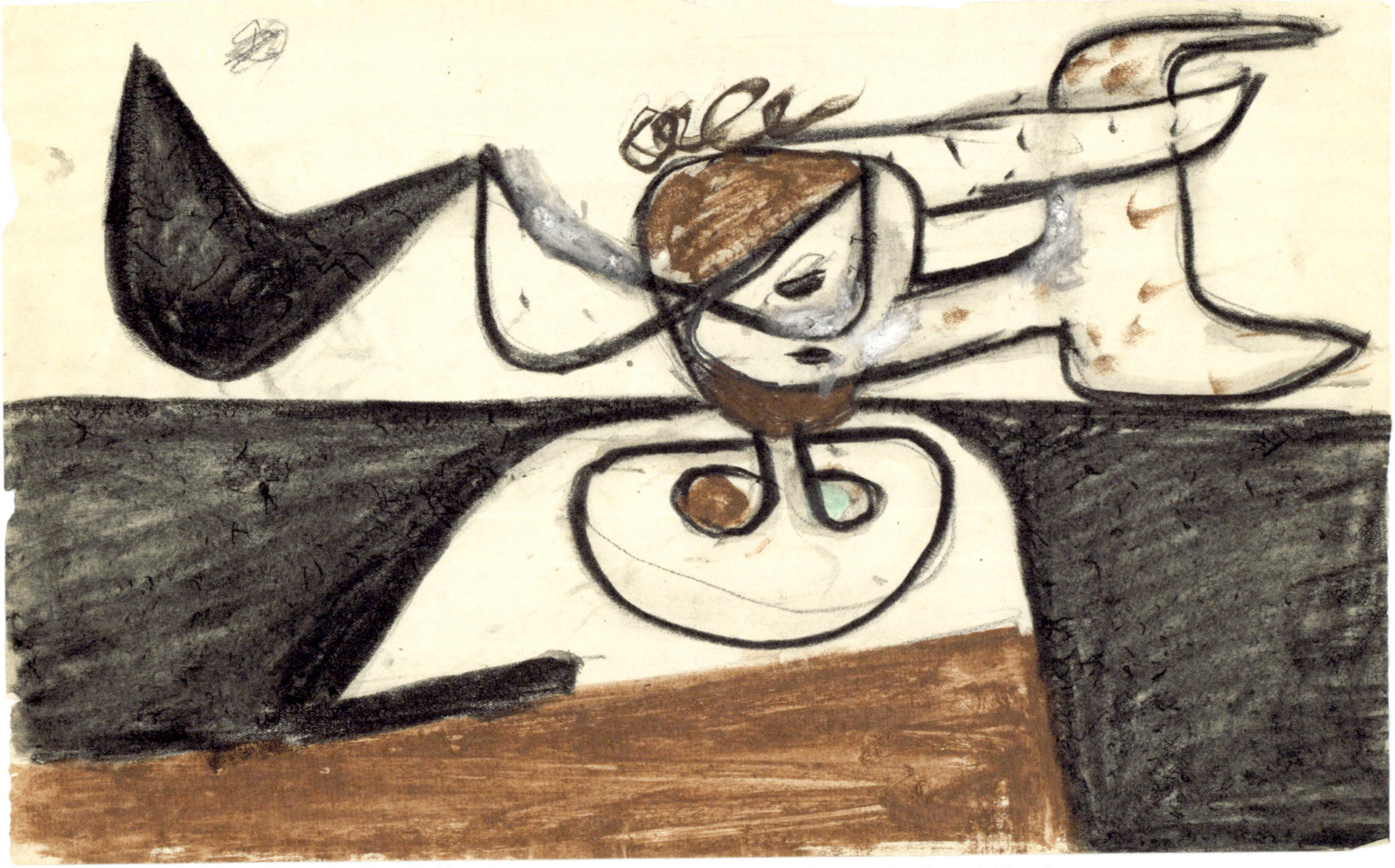

LE CORBUSIER, *étude sur le thème des taureaux - Taureau I*, c. 1952. Graphite pencil and pastel diluted with water on paper, 21.3 × 34.3 cm. Unsigned, undated. Fondation Le Corbusier ©FLC/ADAGP

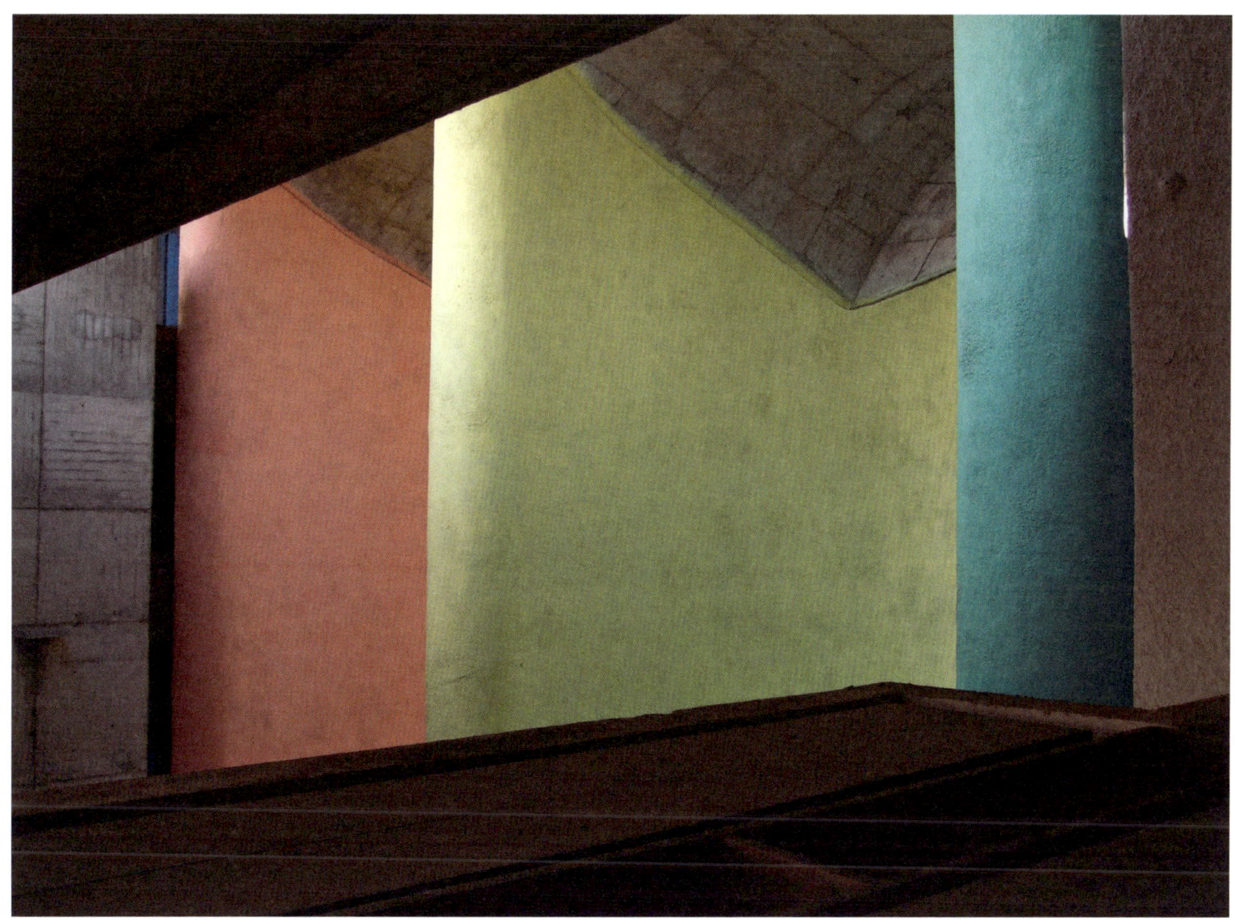

LE CORBUSIER, Haute-Cour, Chandigarh, India, 1952–1955. Fondation Le Corbusier ©FLC/ADAGP

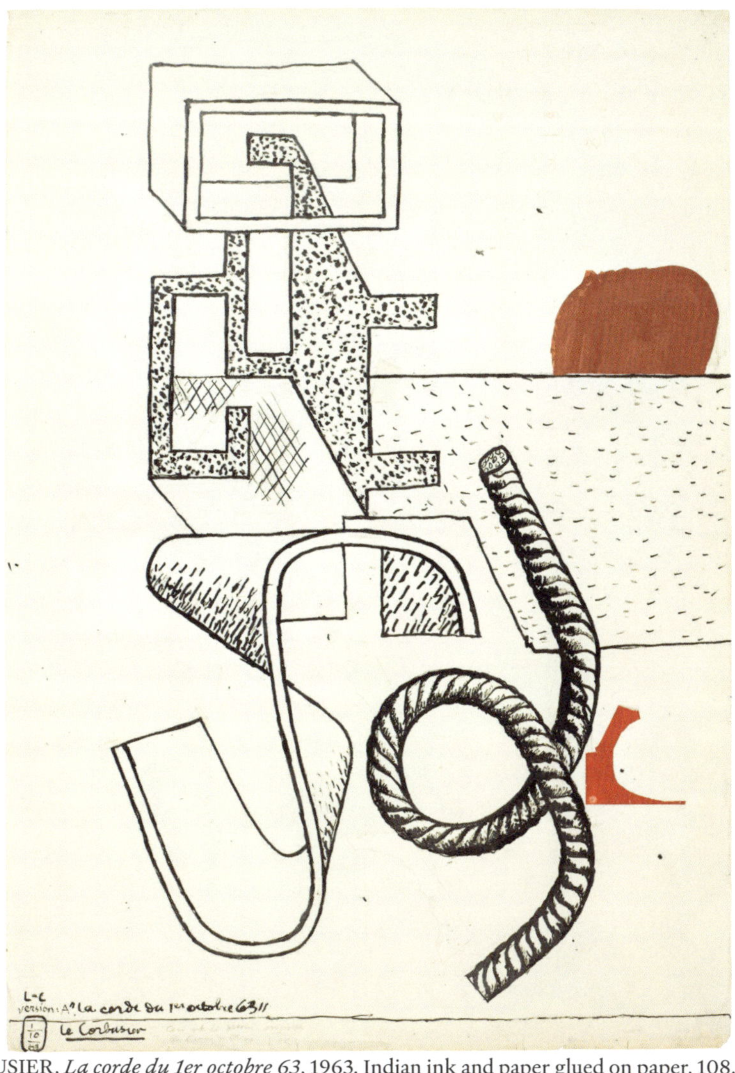

LE CORBUSIER, *La corde du 1er octobre 63*, 1963. Indian ink and paper glued on paper, 108.2 × 75 cm.
Monogrammed and dated lower right "L-C / 1/10/63." Fondation Le Corbusier ©FLC/ADAGP

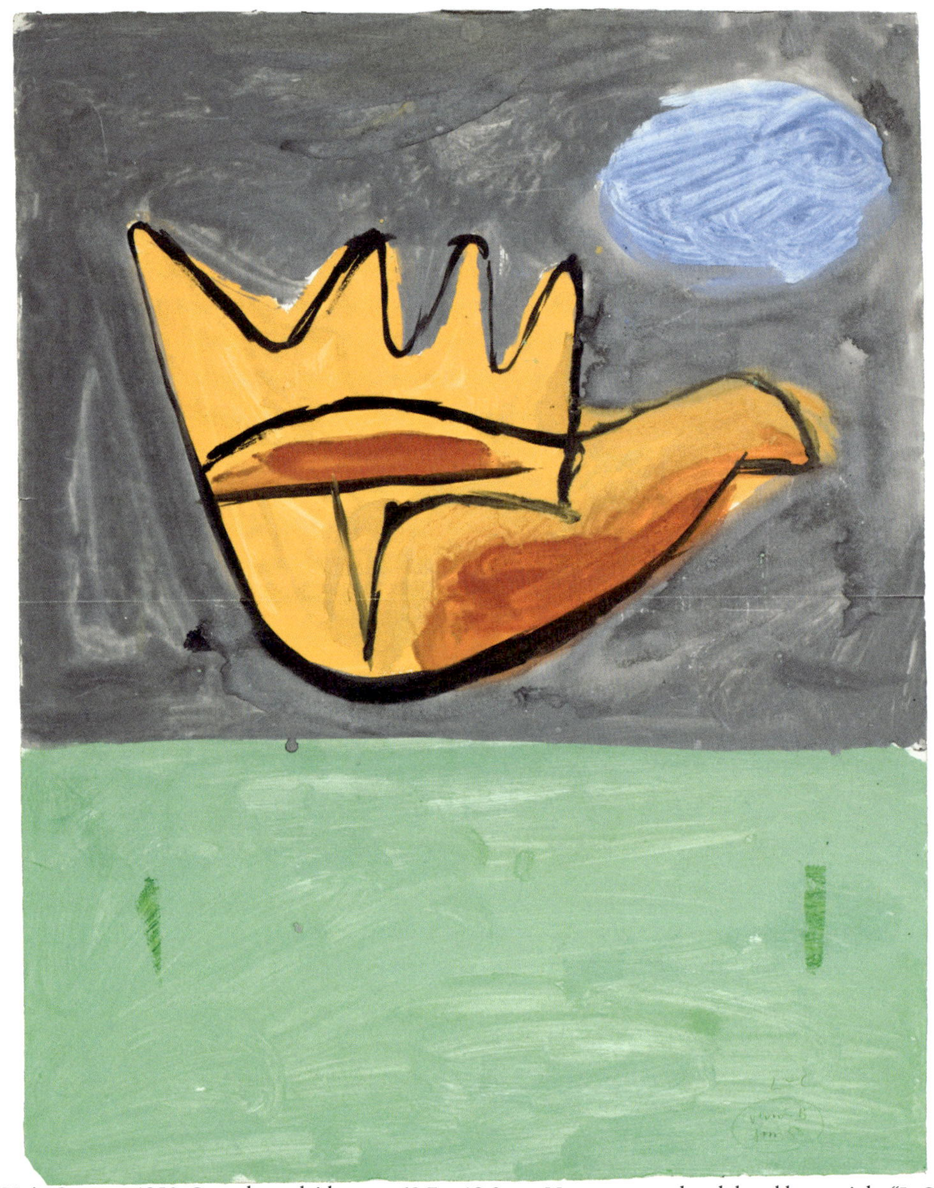

LE CORBUSIER, *La Main Ouverte*, 1950. Gouache on laid paper, 62.7 × 48.3 cm. Monogrammed and dated lower right “L-C / version B / juin 50.” Fondation Le Corbusier ©FLC/ADAGP

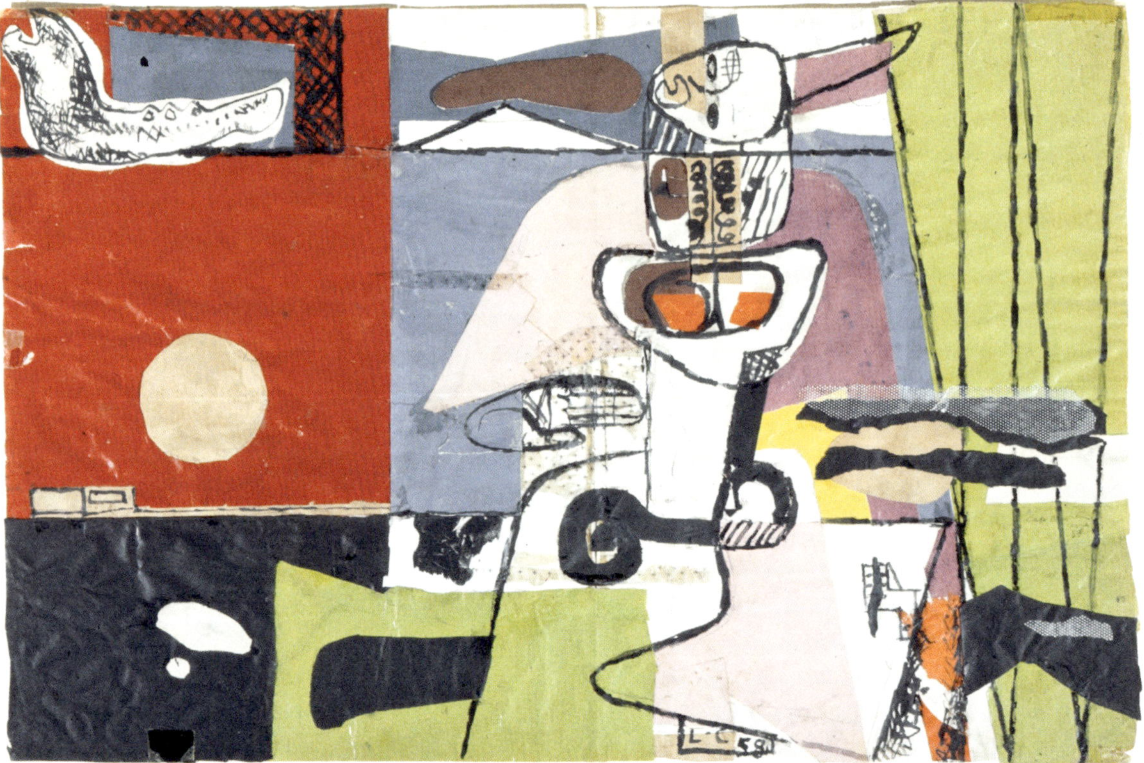

LE CORBUSIER, *Le taureau trivalent (projet pour tapisserie)*, 1958. Graphite pencil, black ink, gouache, glued paper and zipaton on paper. Monogrammed and dated lower center “L-C / 58”; dated lower right “Cap Martin / août / 58.” Fondation Le Corbusier ©FLC/ADAGP

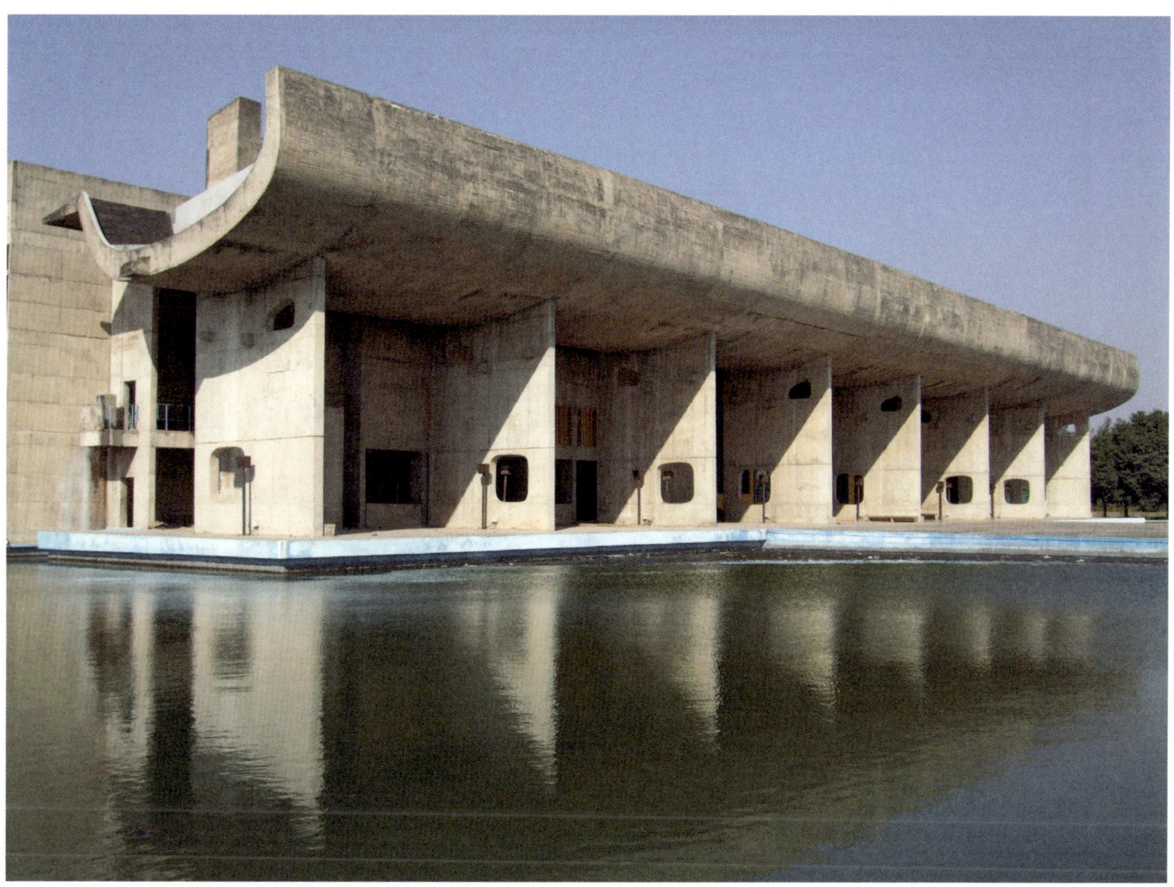

LE CORBUSIER, Palais de l'assemblée, Chandigarh, India, 1951–1963. Fondation Le Corbusier ©FLC/ADAGP

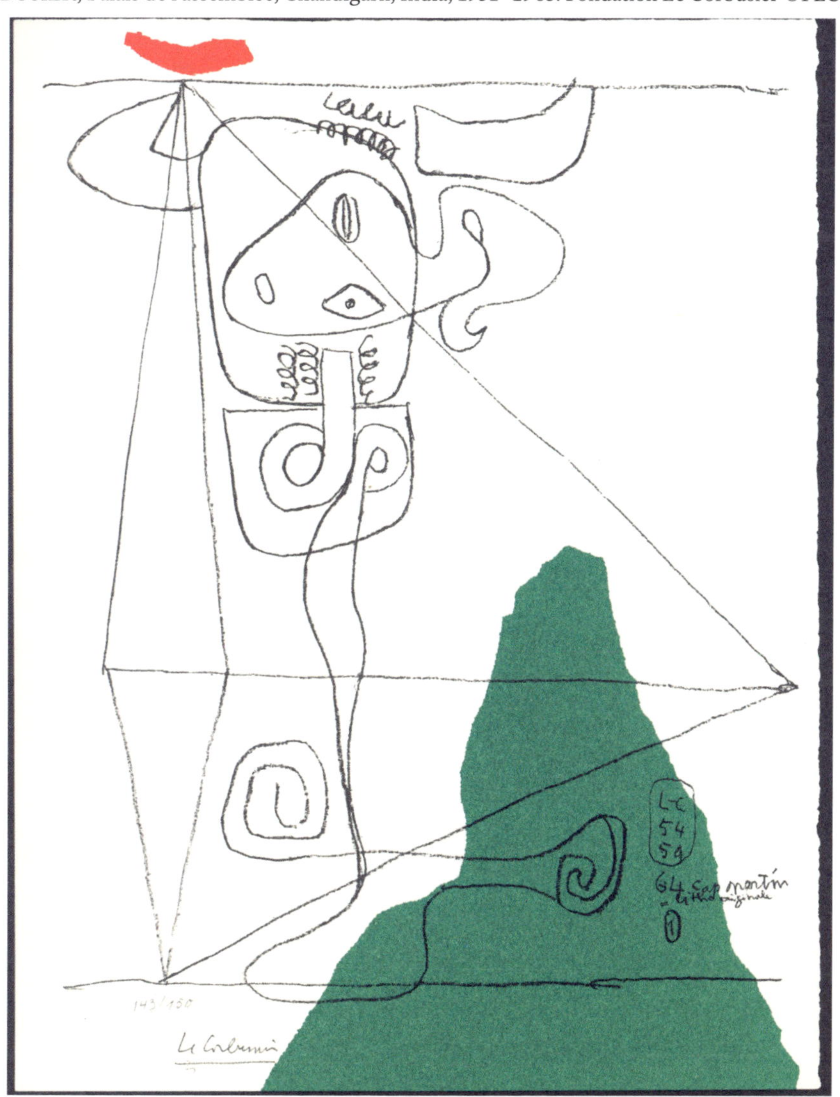

LE CORBUSIER, *Taureau I*, 1954–1964. Original lithography, 72 × 54 cm. Monogrammed and dated lower right "L-C / 54 / 59 / 64 Cap Martin." Fondation Le Corbusier ©FLC/ADAGP

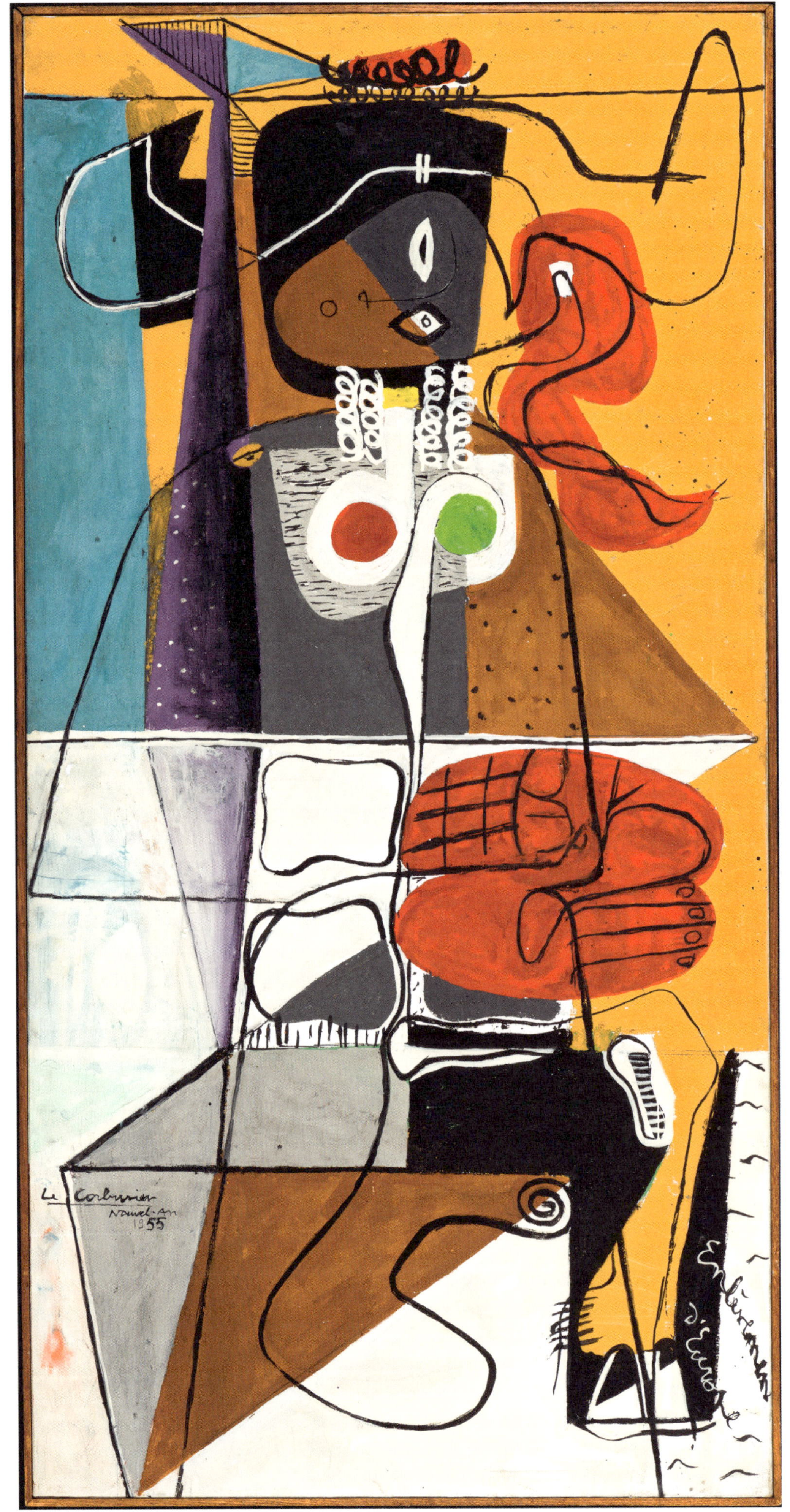

LE CORBUSIER, *Taureau X*, 1955. Oil on canvas, 195 × 97 cm. Signed and dated lower right "Le Corbusier / Nouvel-An / 1955."
Fondation Le Corbusier ©FLC/ADAGP

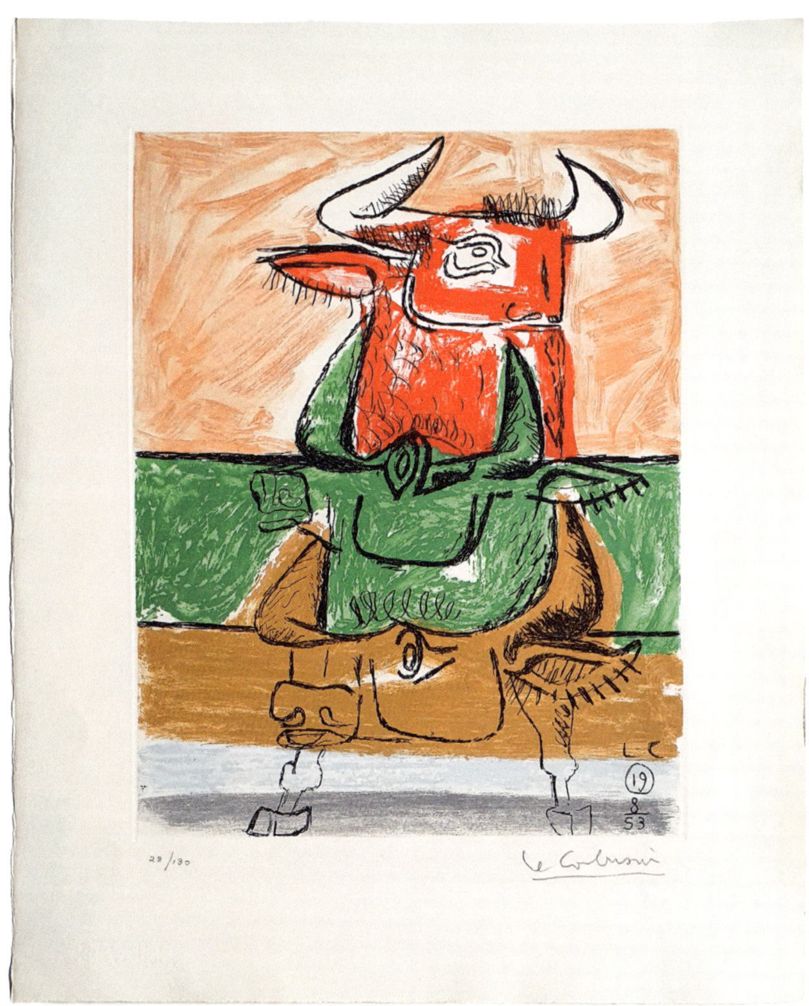

LE CORBUSIER, *Taureau*, 1965. Plate 19 from the album *Unité*, 1953. Fondation Le Corbusier ©FLC/ADAGP

PLAN OF NEW CAPITAL PUNJAB

INDEX TO NUMBERS

LEGEND

CHANDIGARH

DRG No. 2/6
PUNJAB CAPITAL PROJECT
SIMLA. PUNJAB. INDIA.

29052

FONDATION LE CORBUSIER

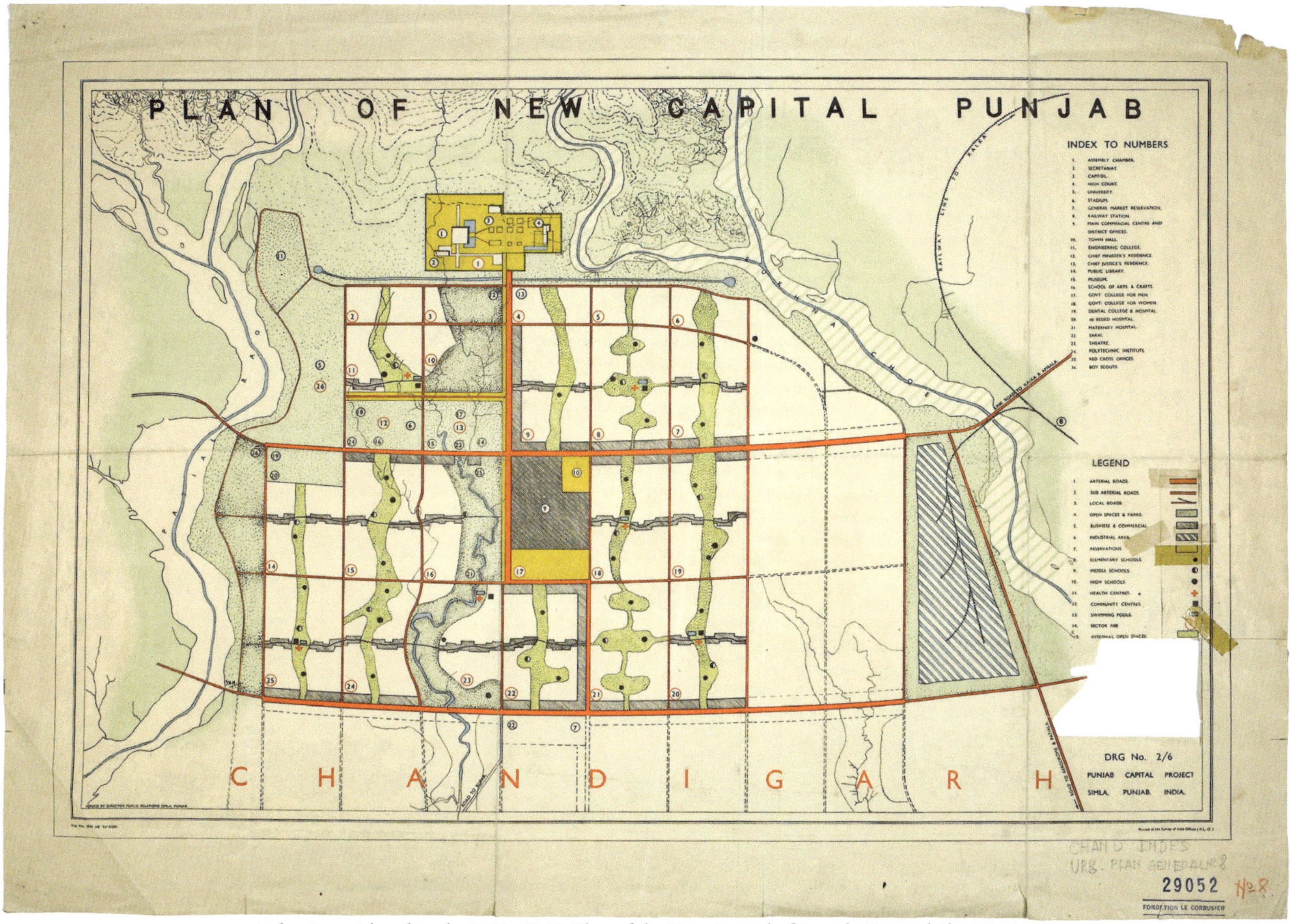

Urbanisme, Chandigarh, 1950–1965. Plan of the New Capital of Punjab, General Plan No. 8.
Color printed on paperboard, 59 × 83 cm. Fondation Le Corbusier ©FLC/ADAGP

PLATES

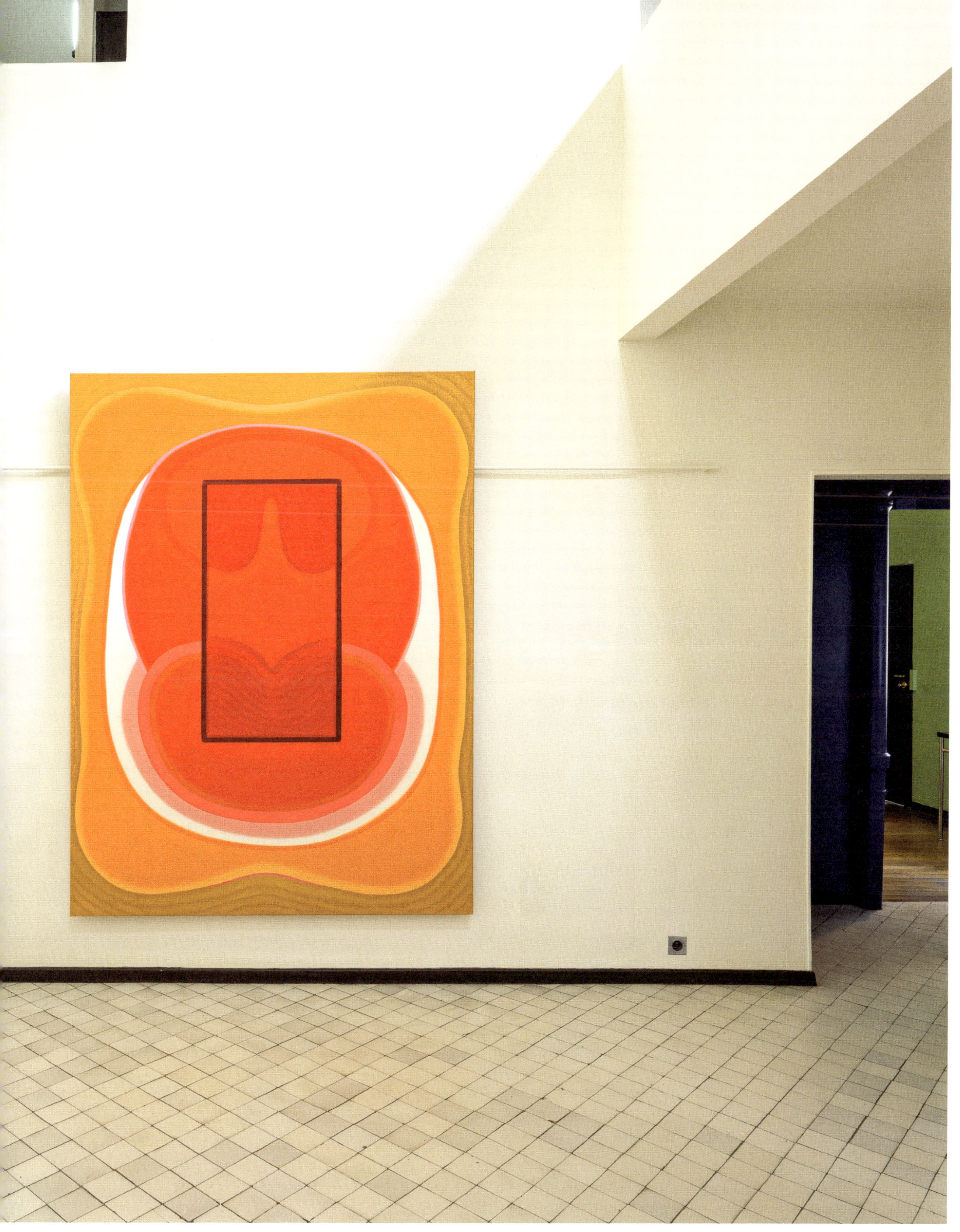

Dahlias of La Tour, oil on linen, 100 × 73 × 2.5 cm (84 × 62 inches)

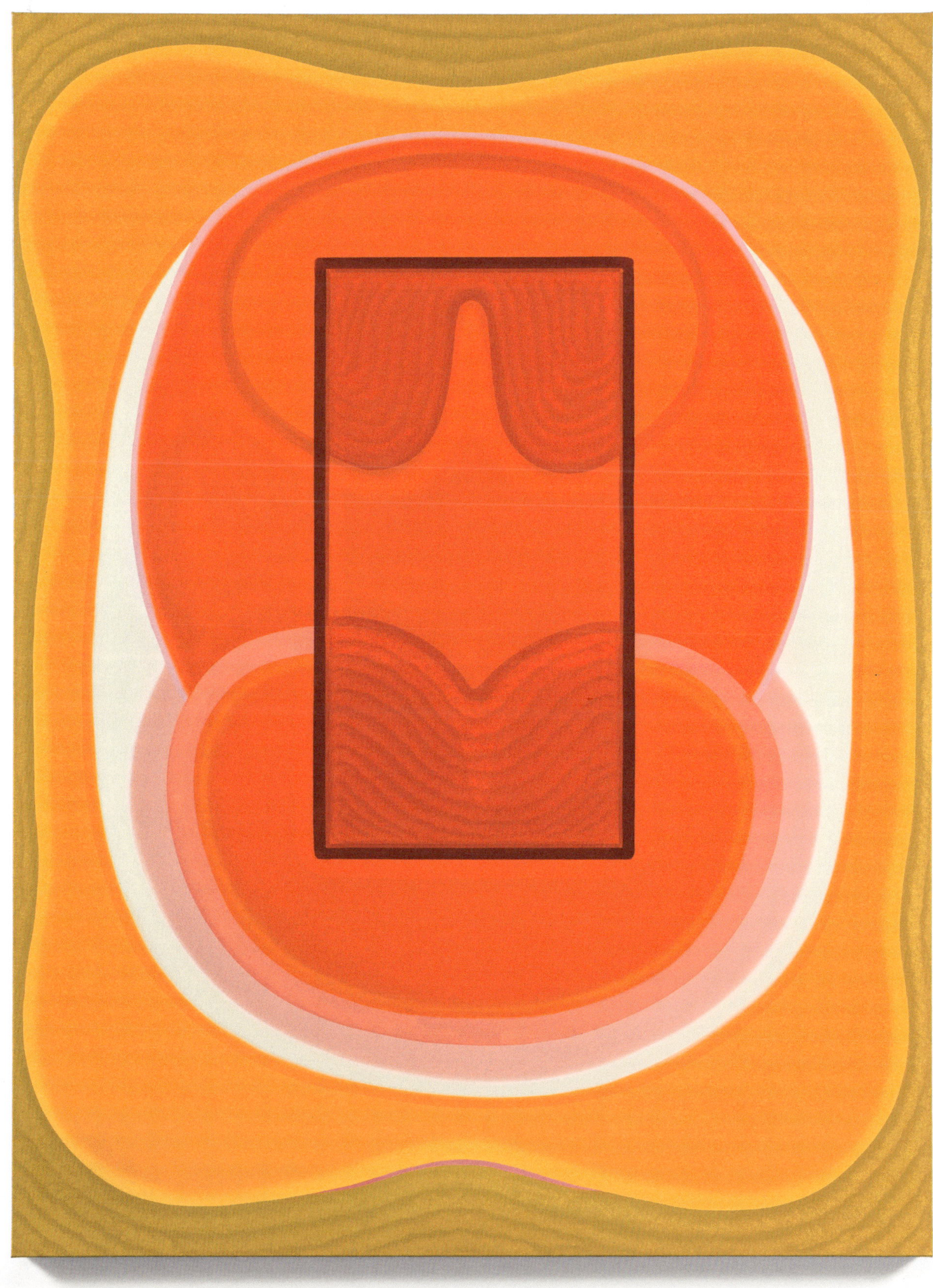

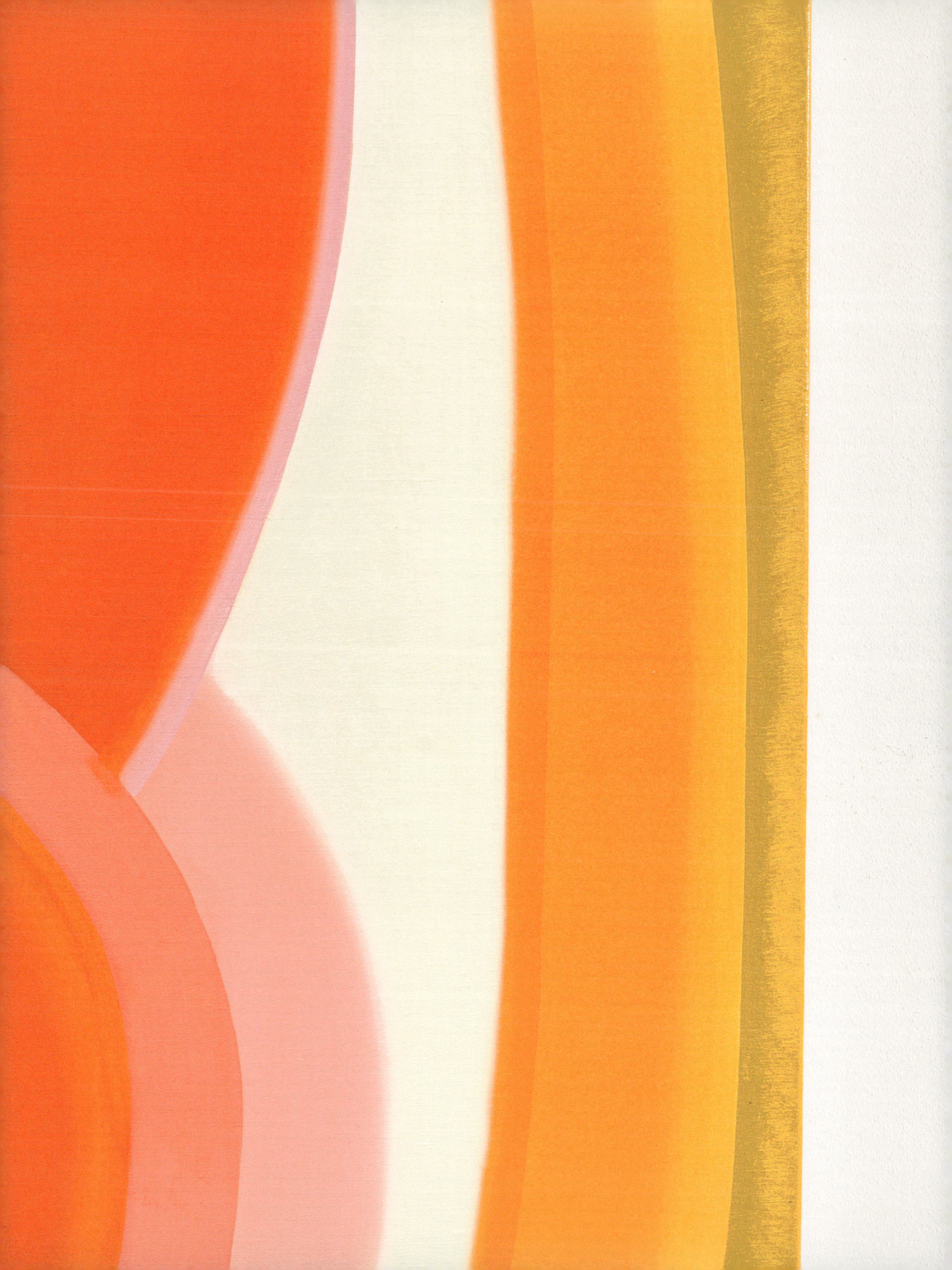

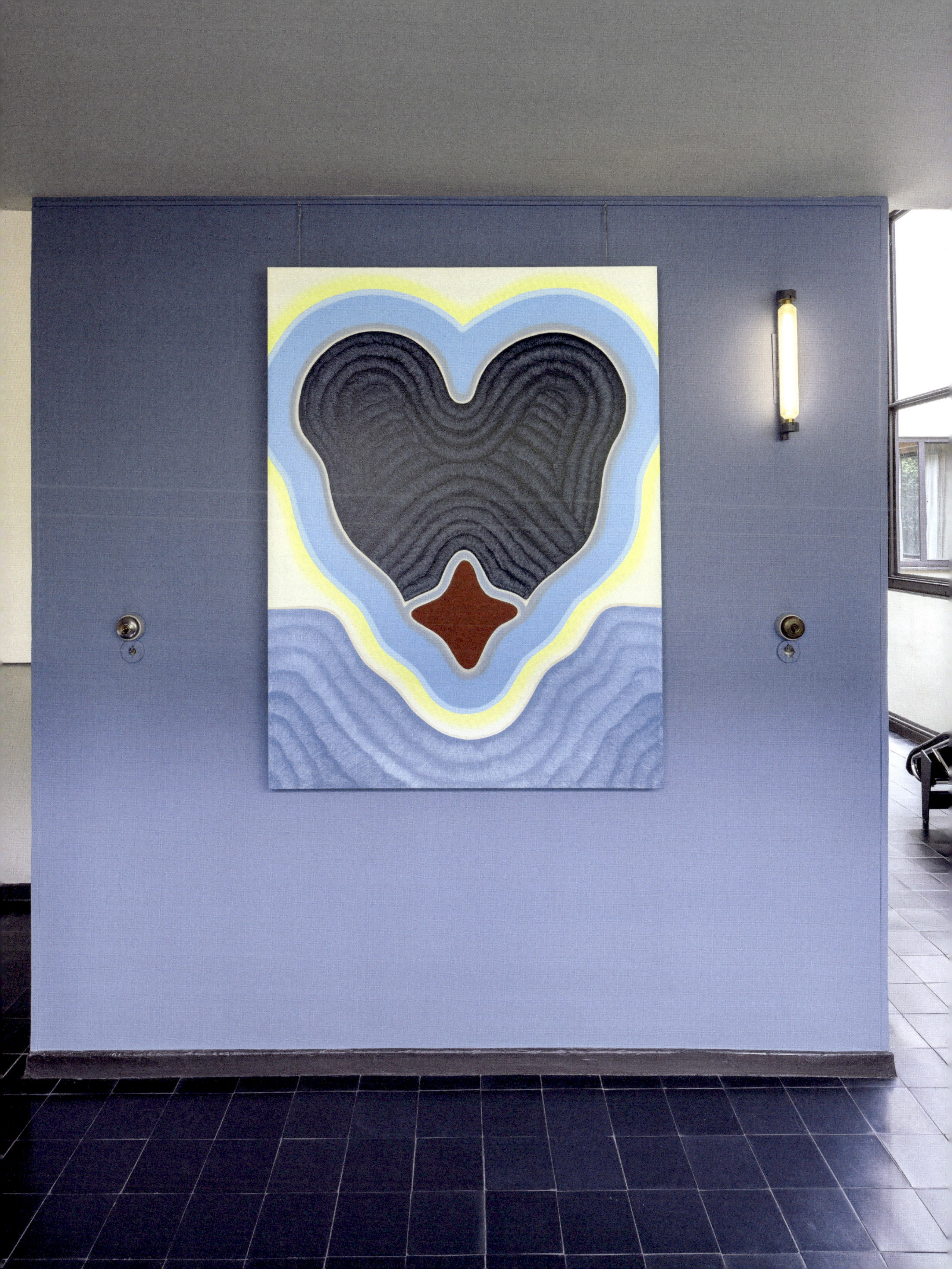

On A Clear Day, oil on linen, 100 × 73 × 2.5 cm (48 × 36 inches)

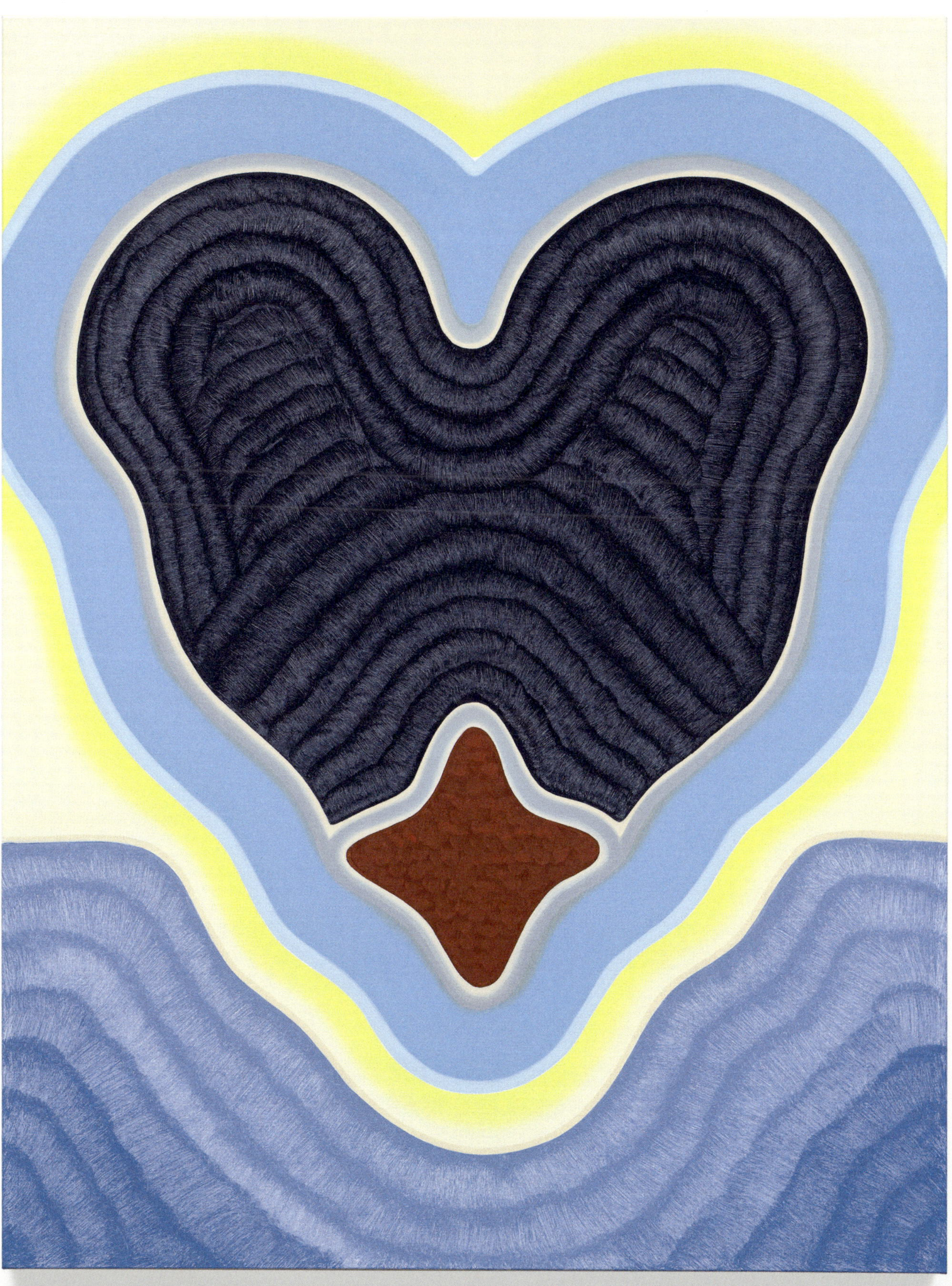

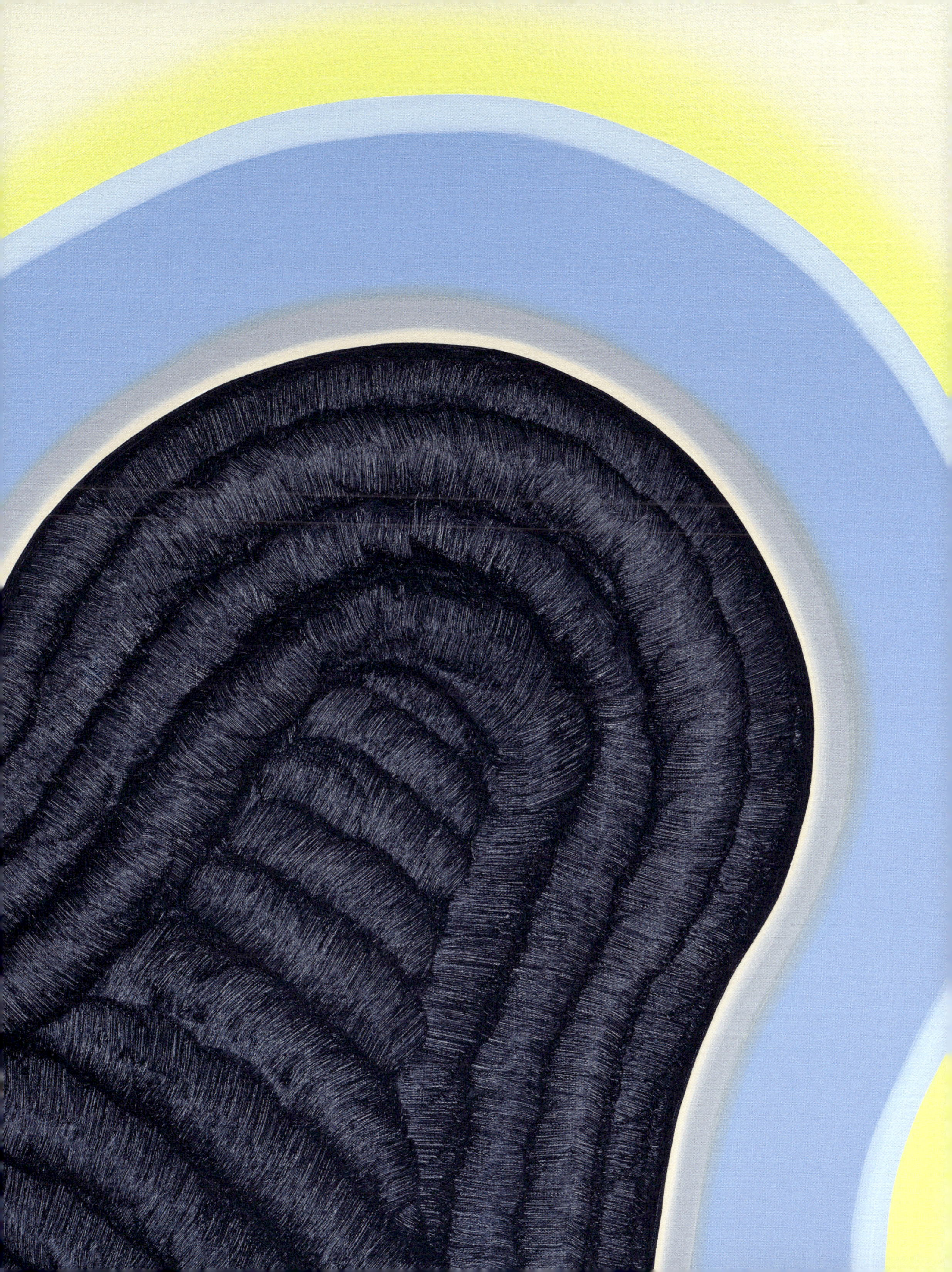

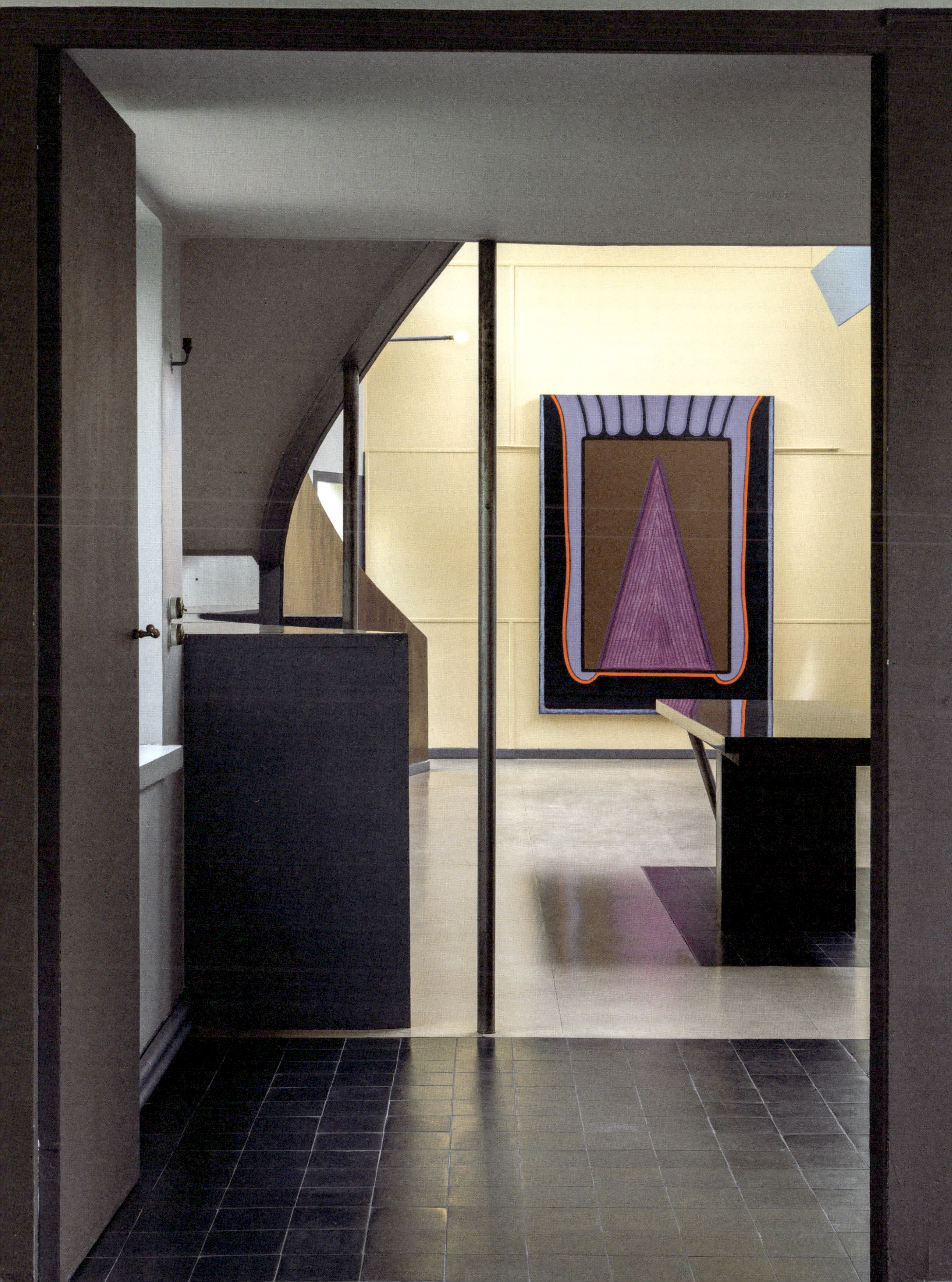

Metronome, oil on linen, 100 × 73 × 2.5 cm (84 × 62 inches)

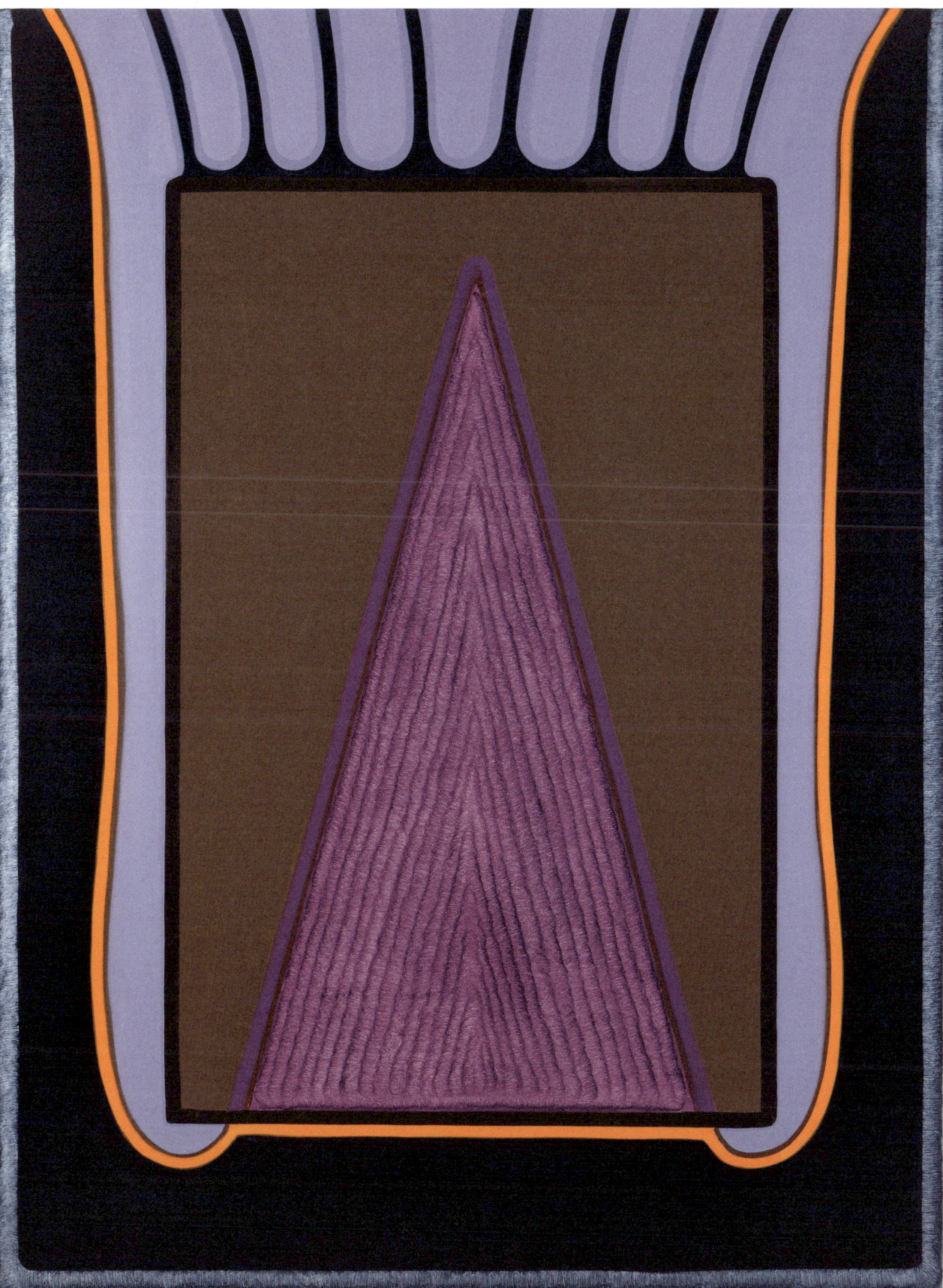

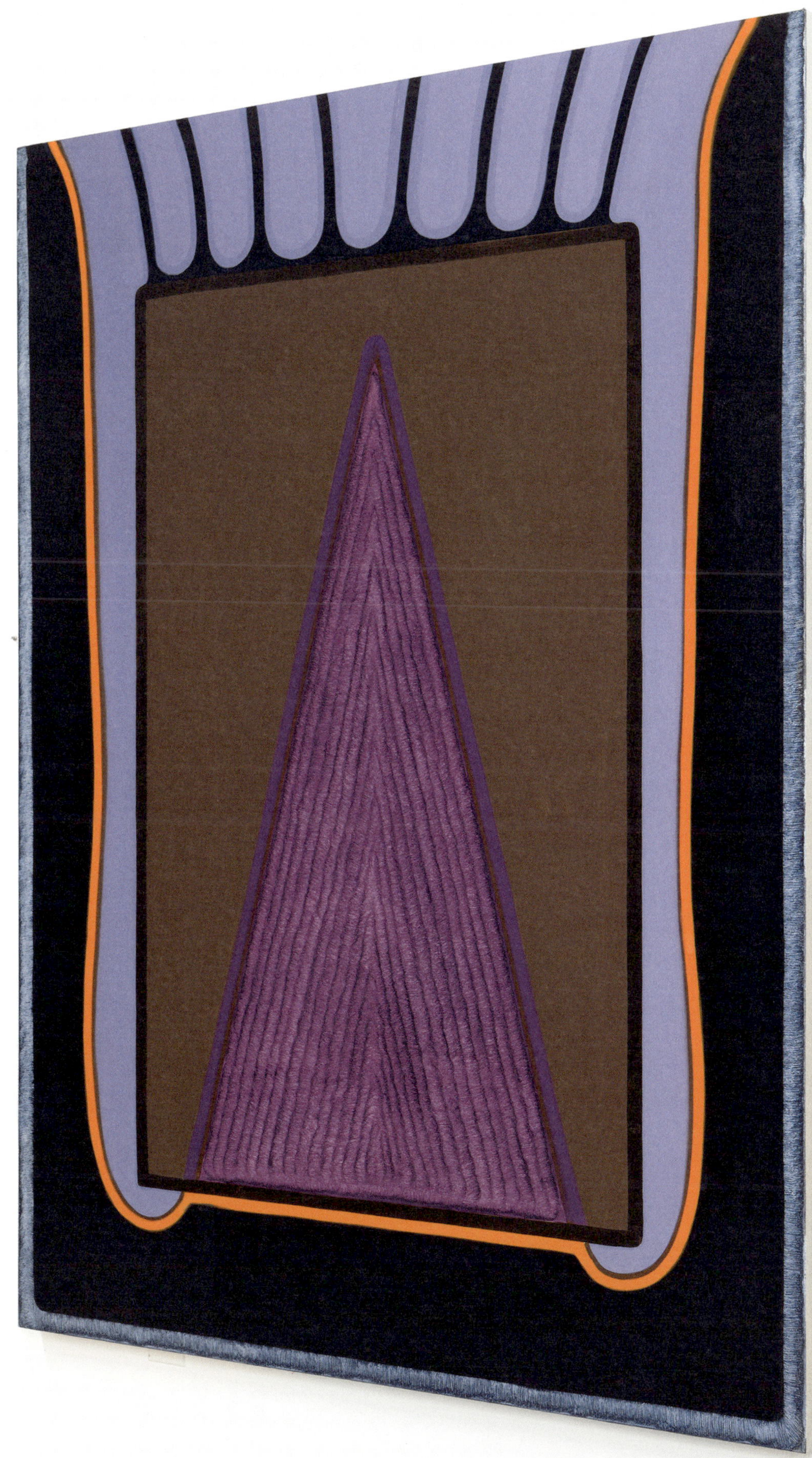

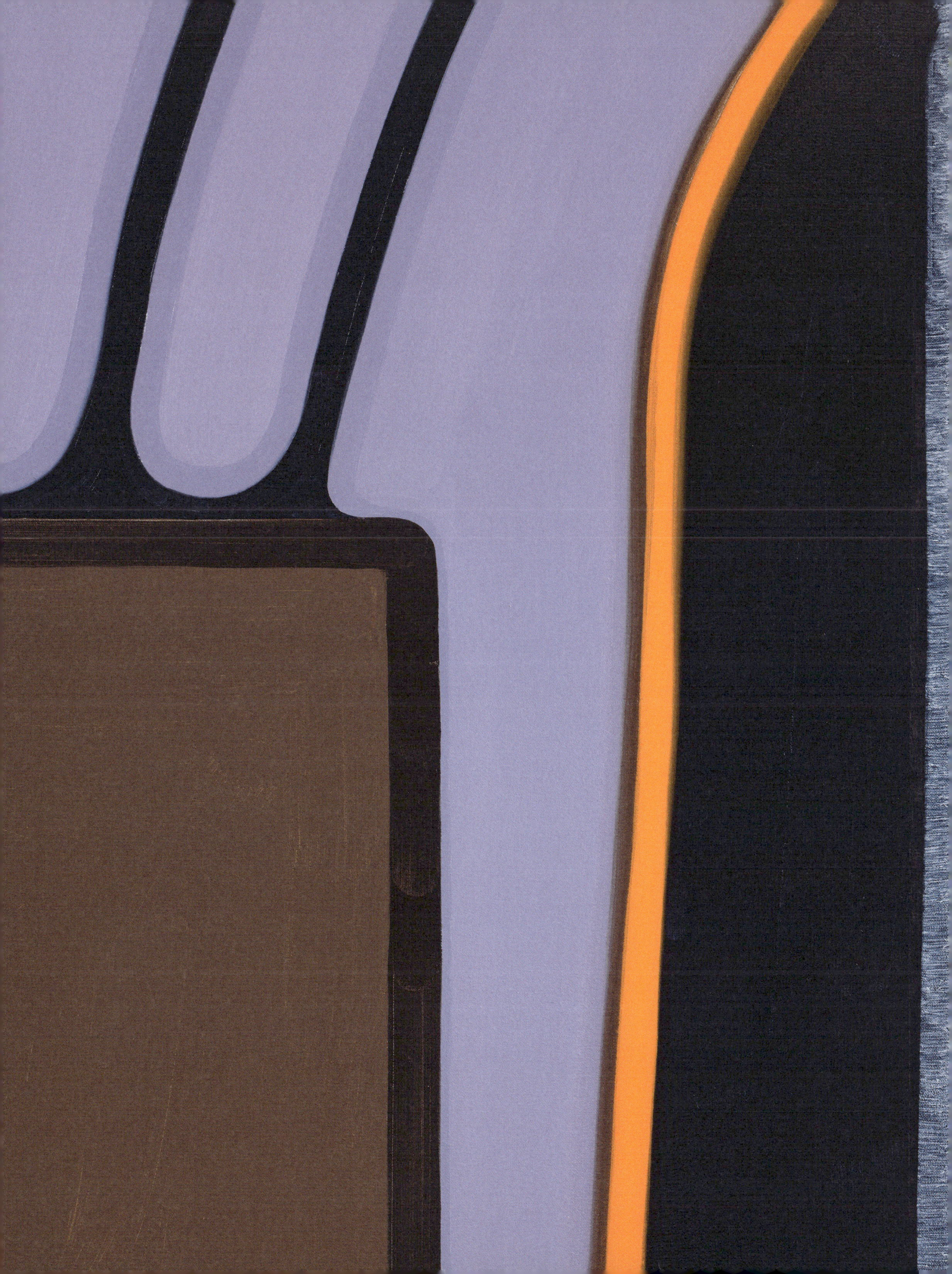

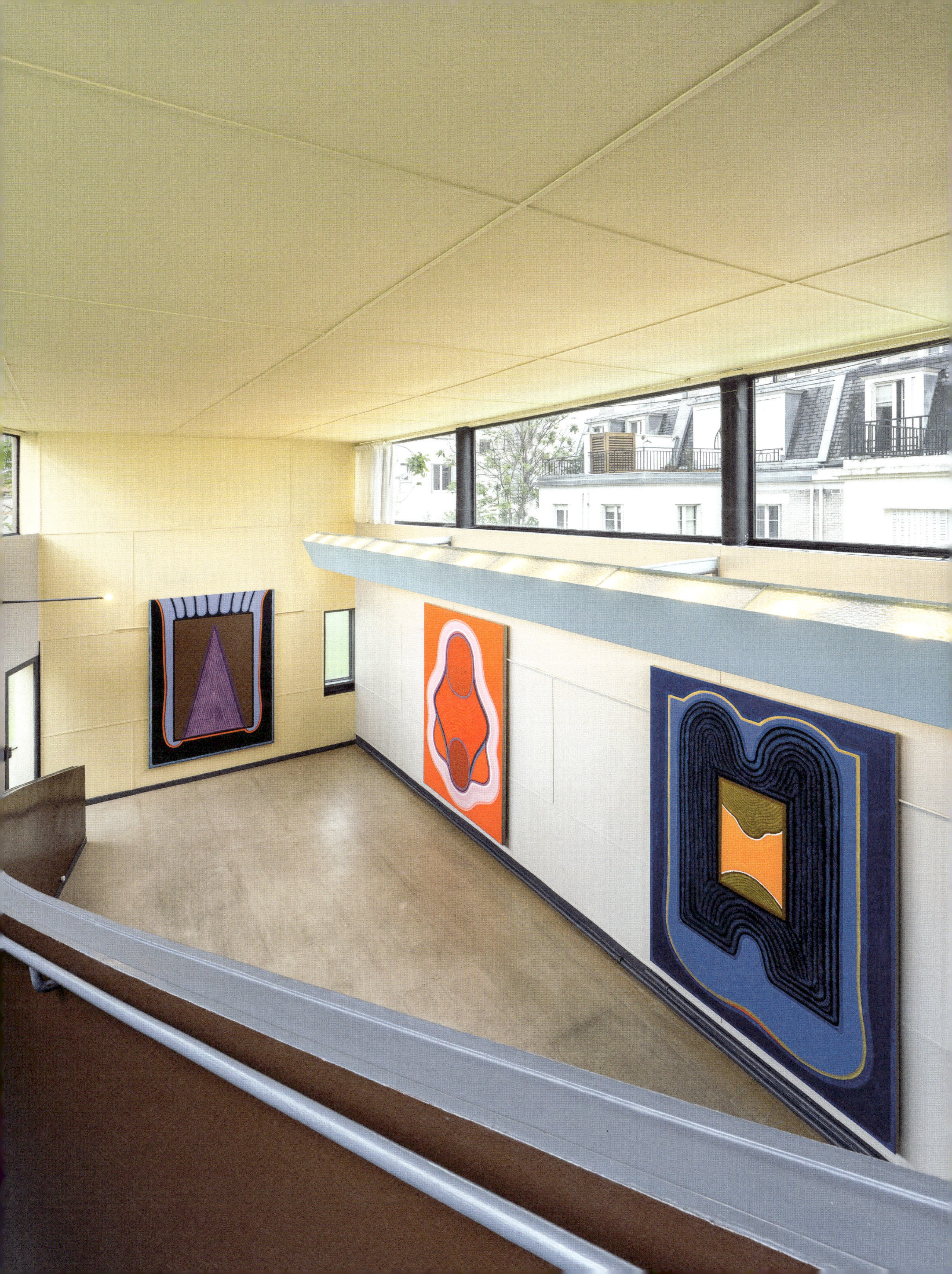

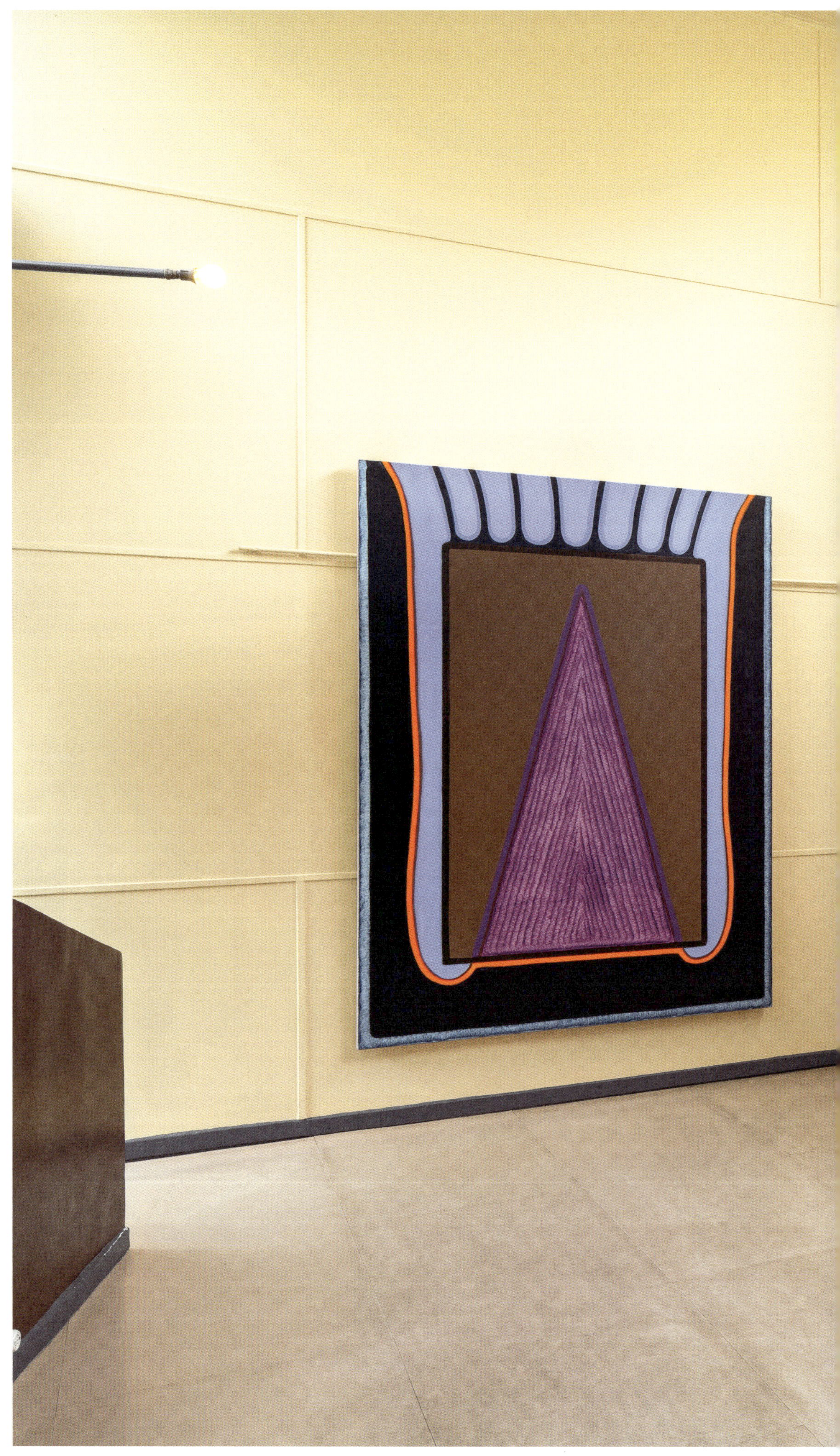

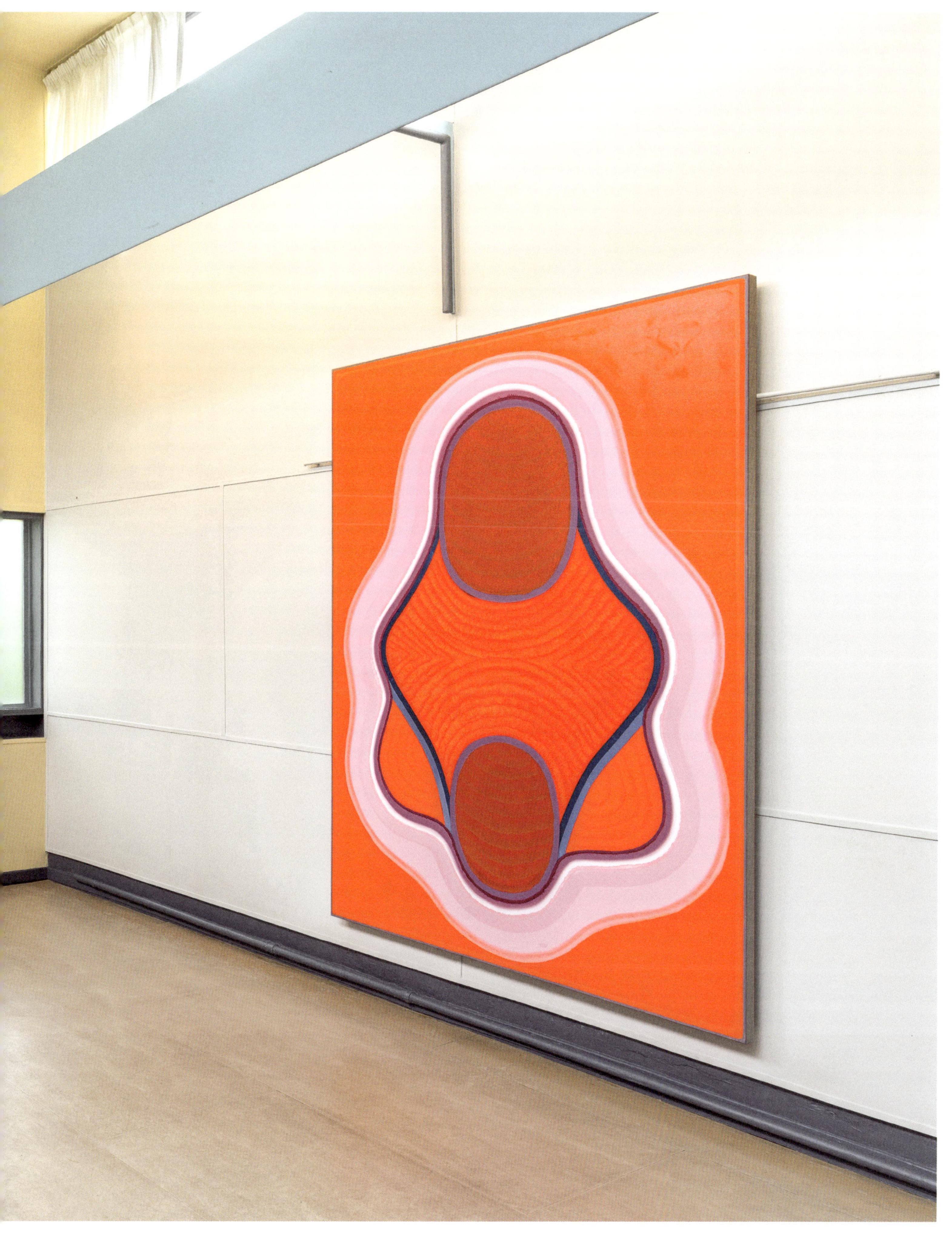

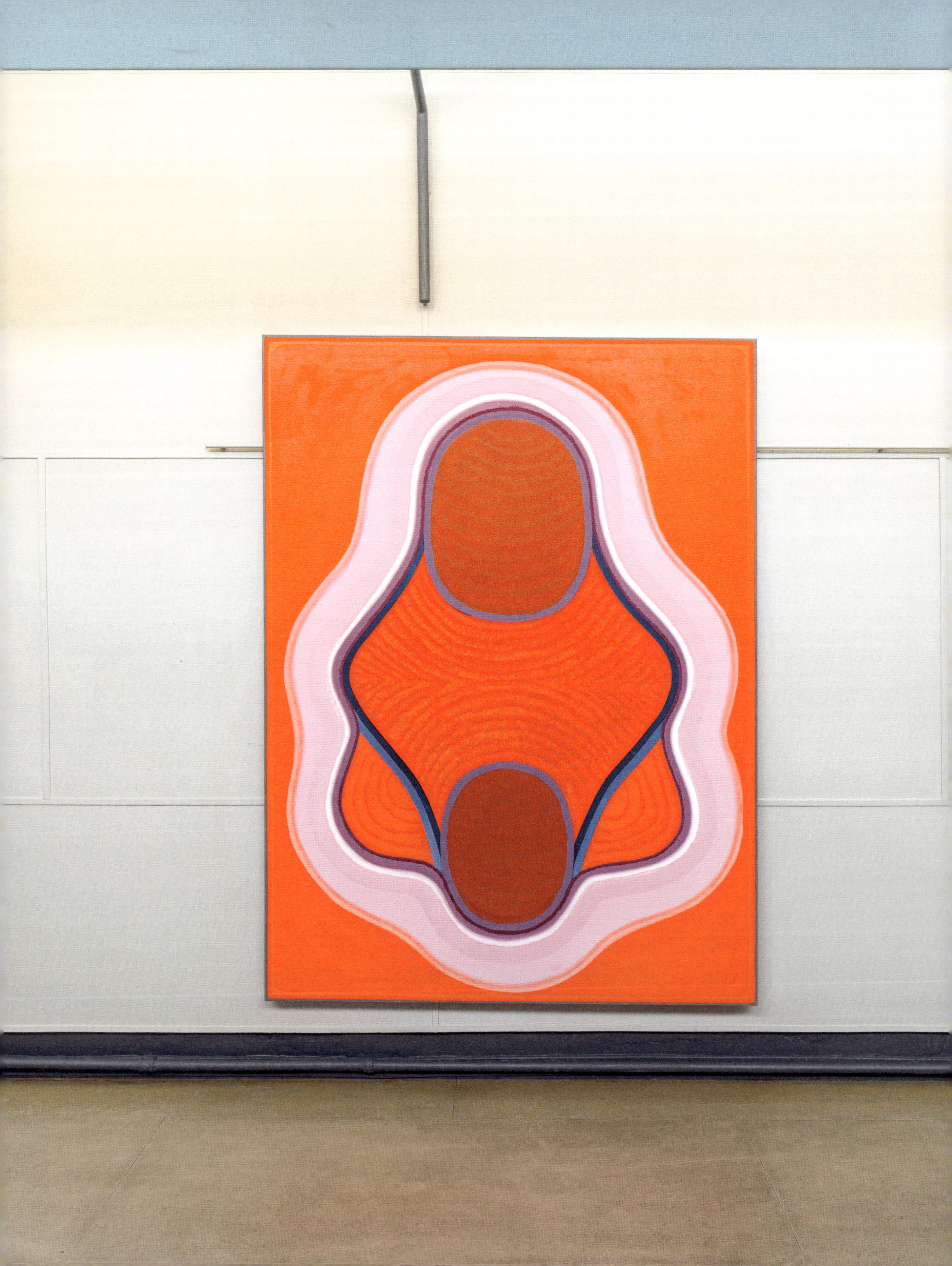

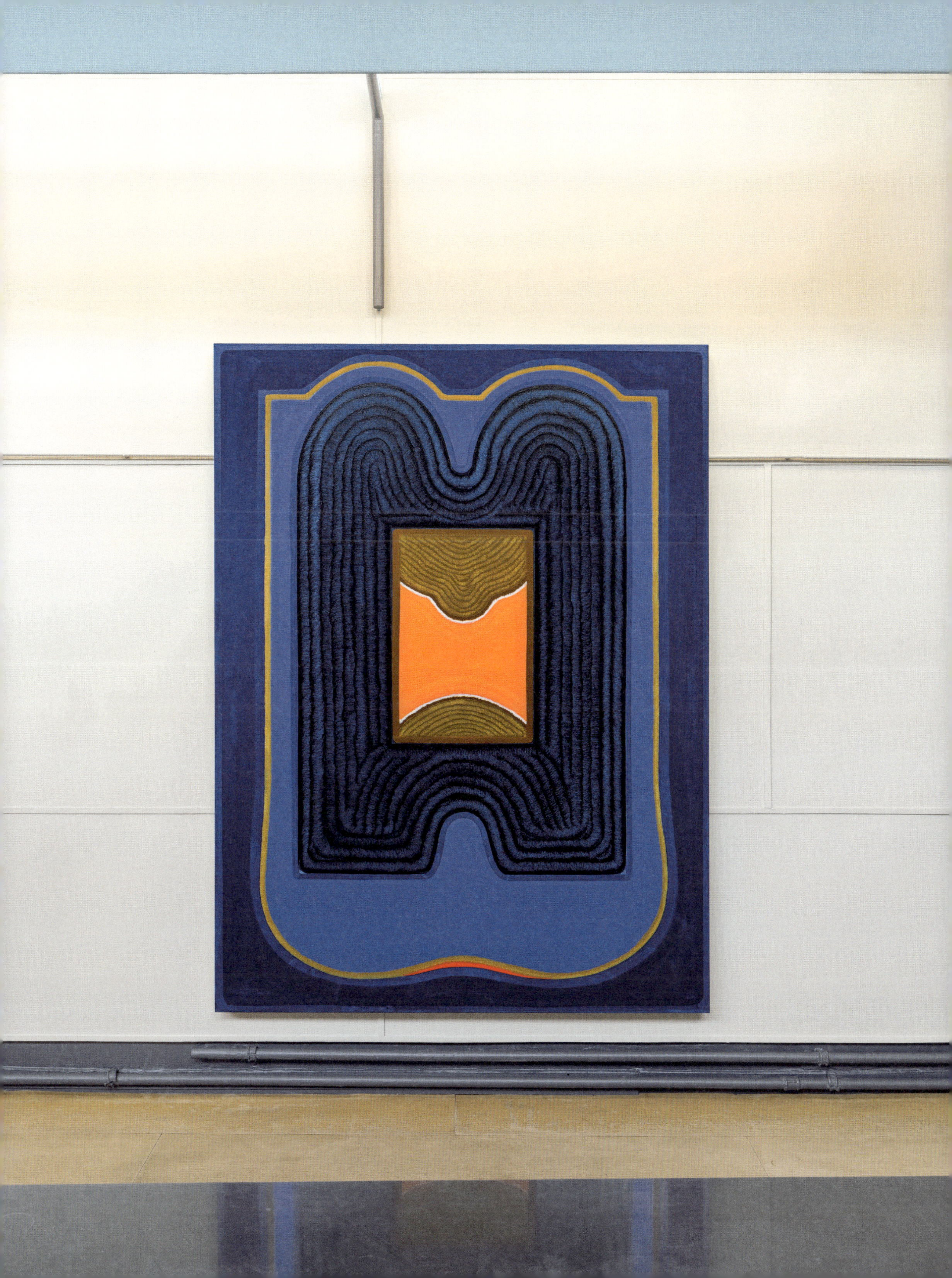

Chandigarh, oil on linen, 100 × 73 × 2.5 cm (84 × 62 inches)

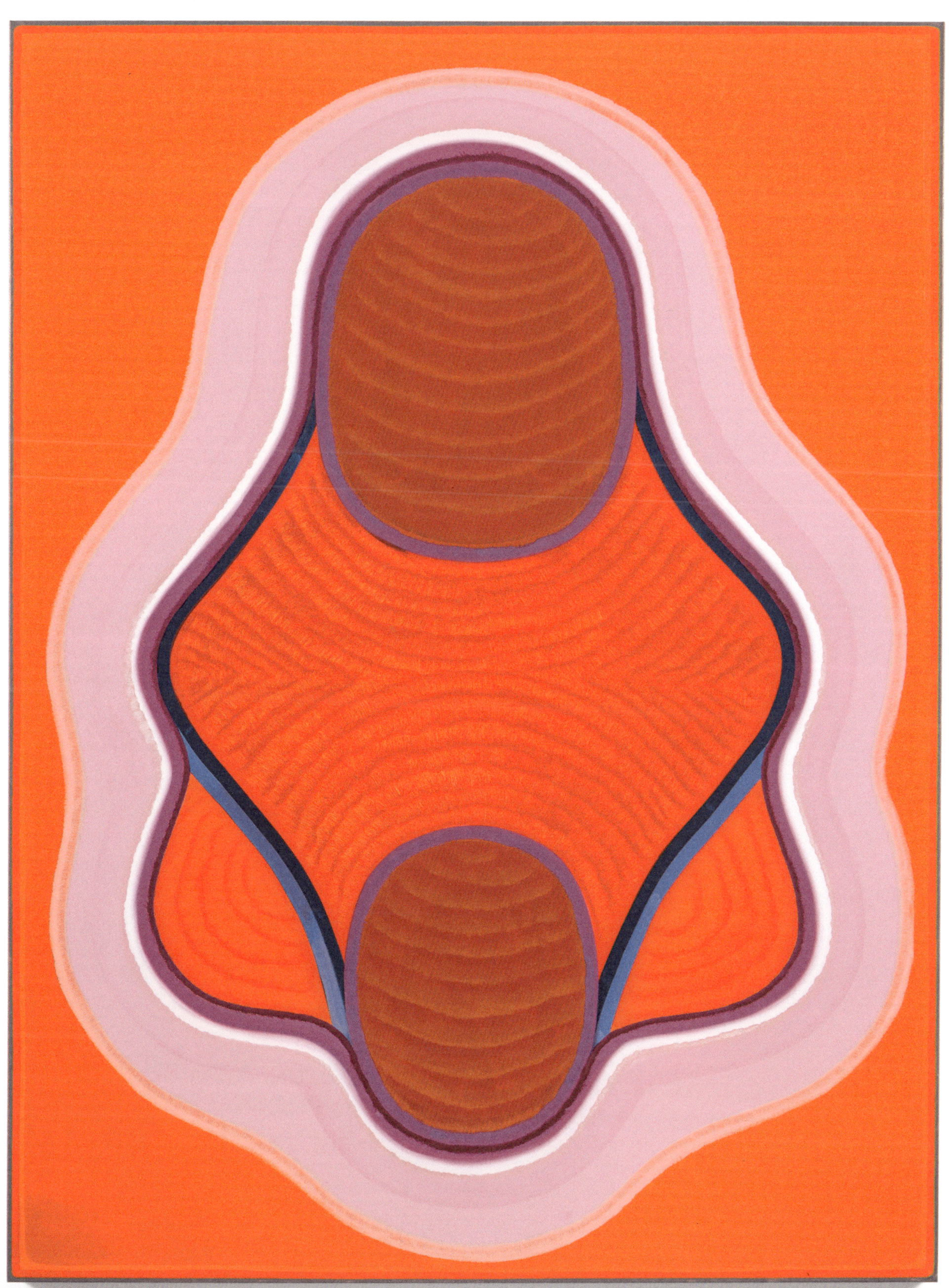

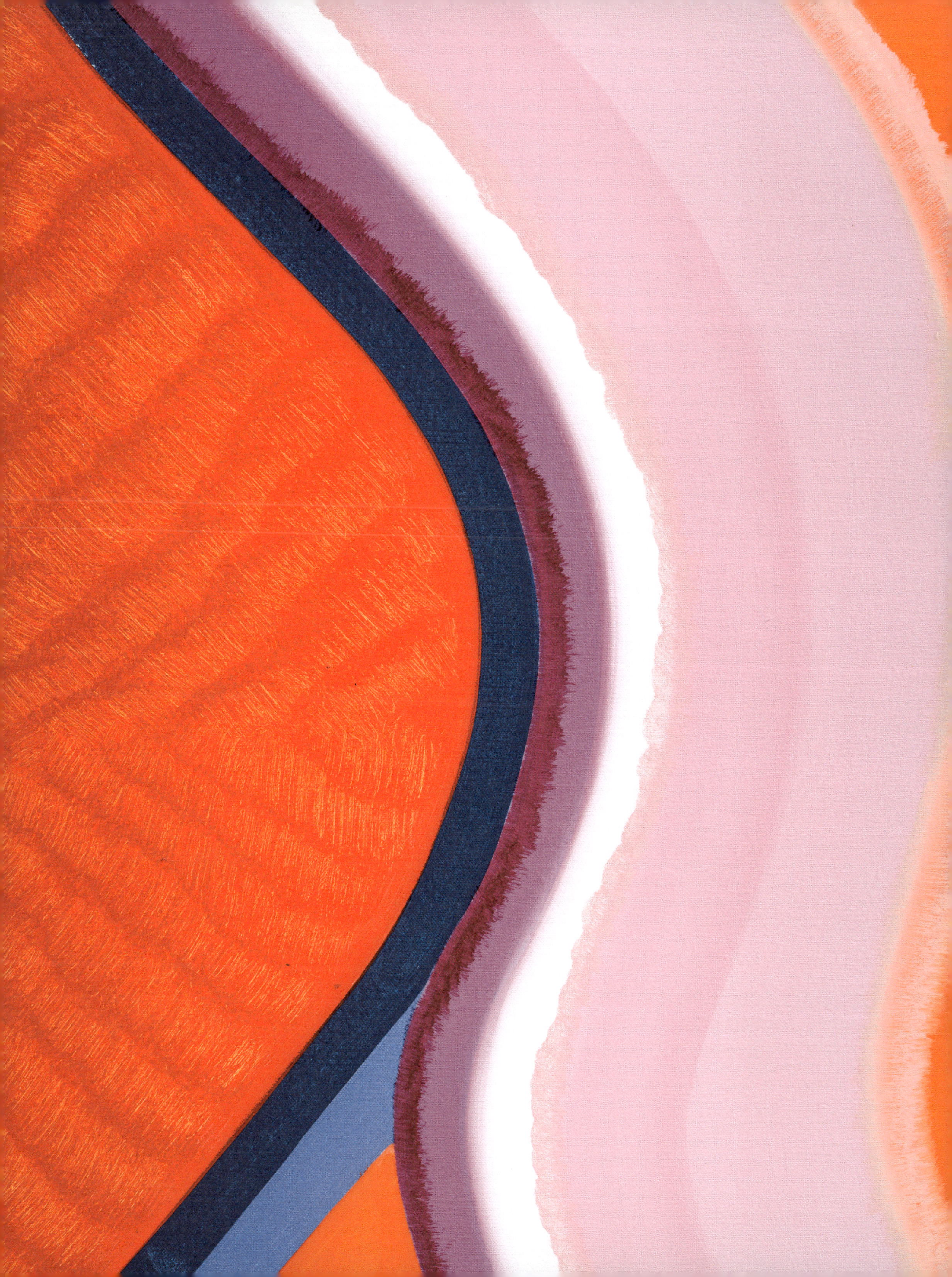

Sukhna Lake, oil on linen, 100 × 73 × 2.5 cm (84 × 62 inches)

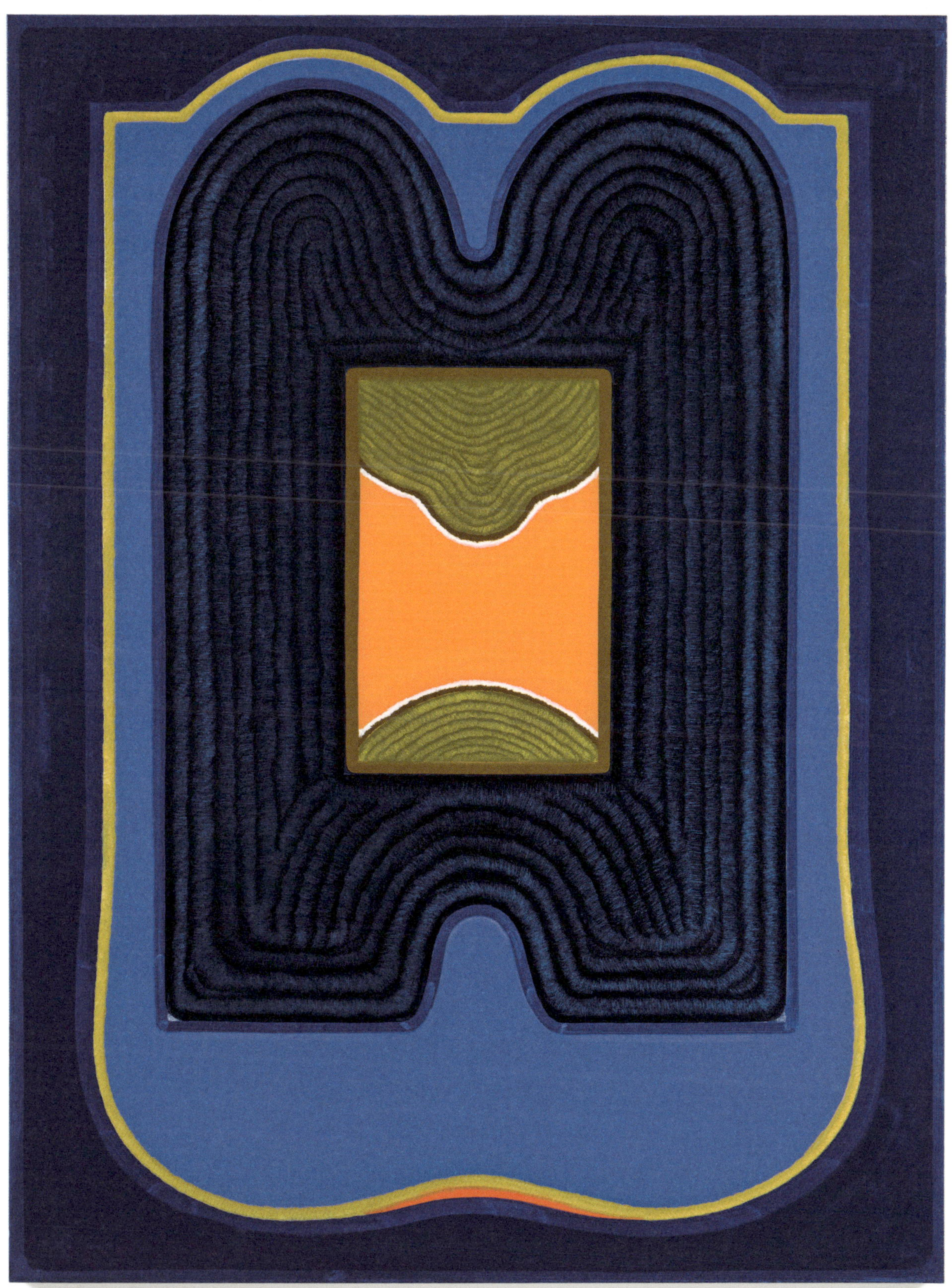

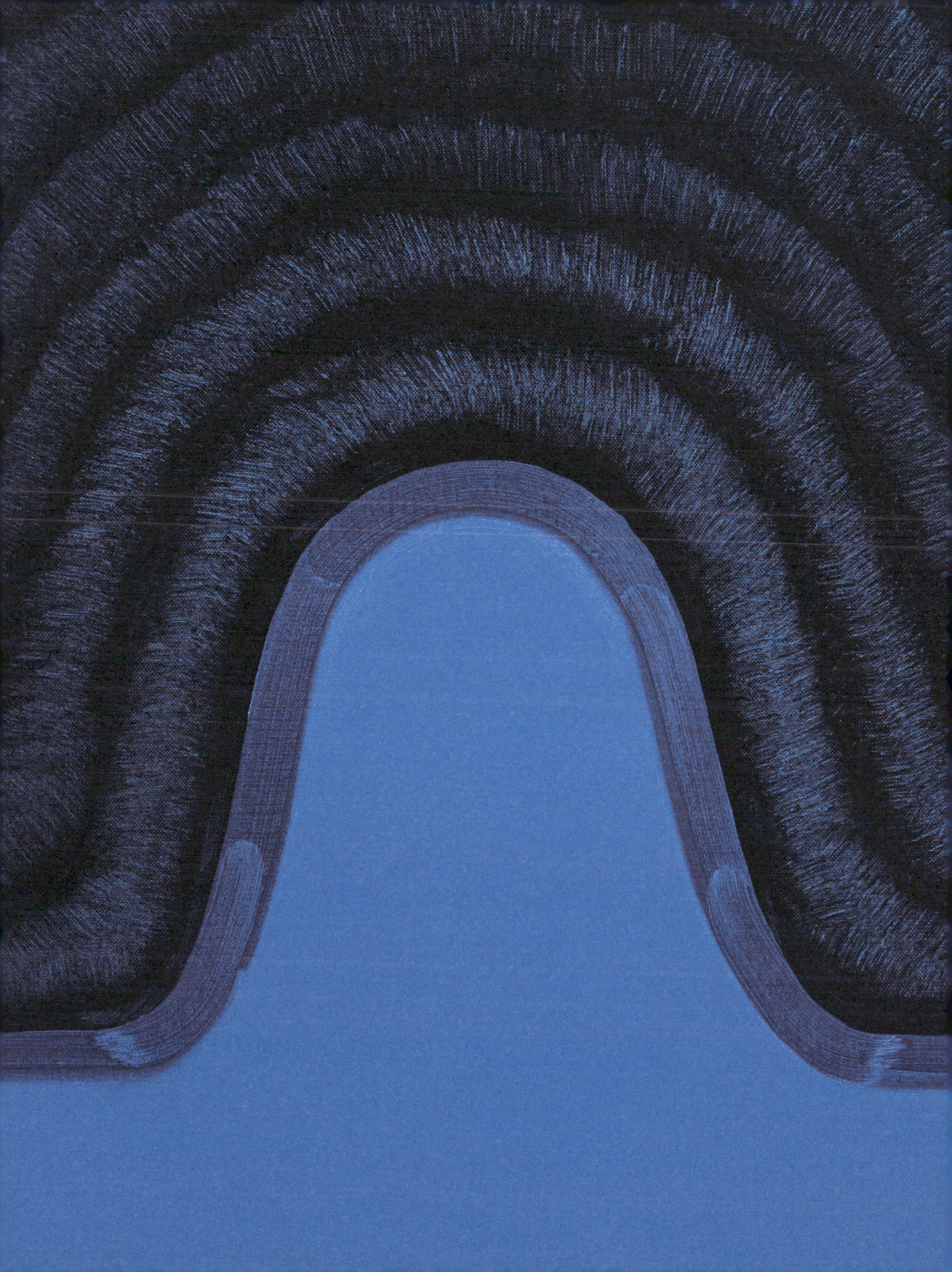

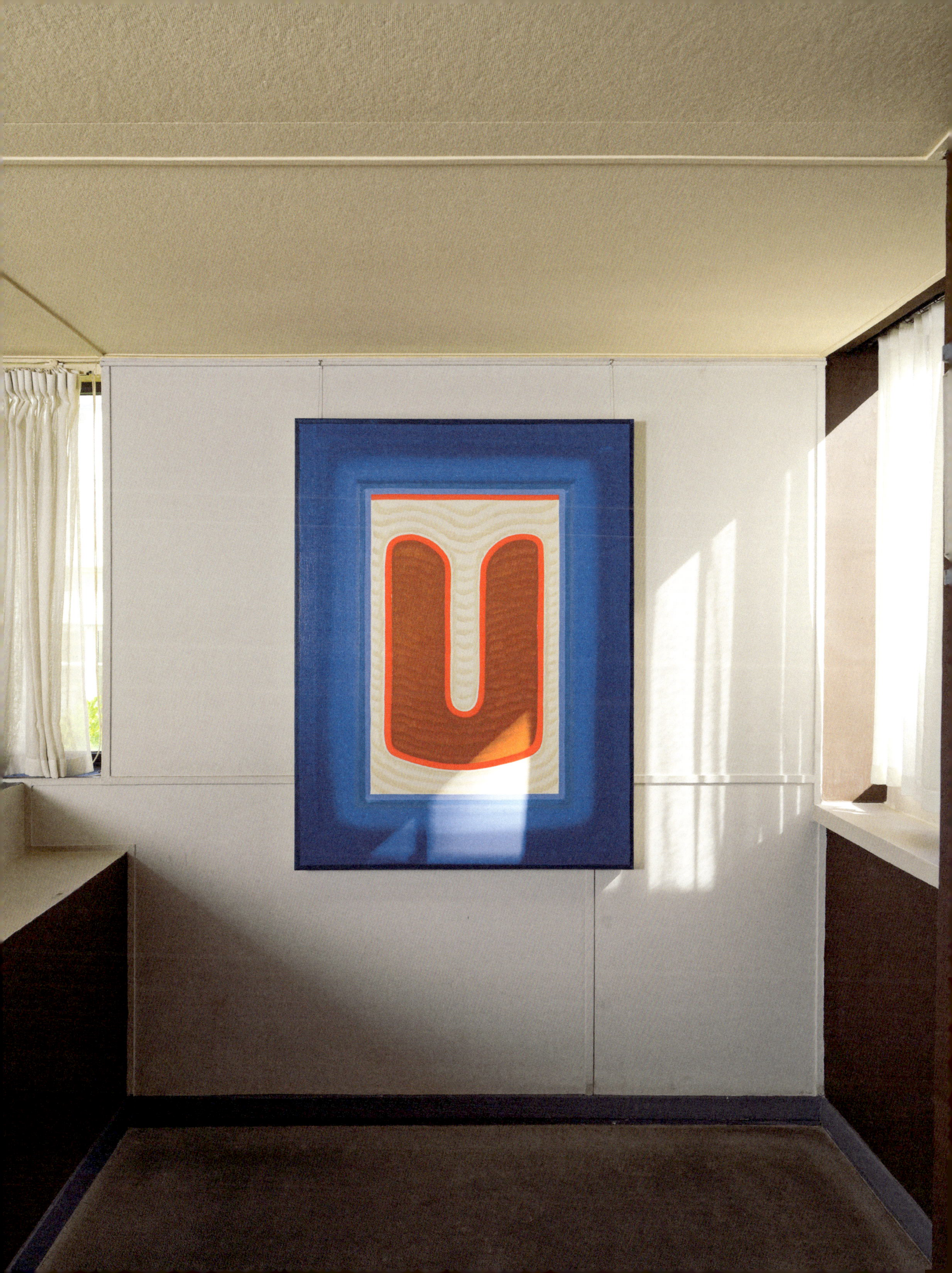

The Architect, oil on linen, 100 × 73 × 2.5 cm (48 × 36 inches)

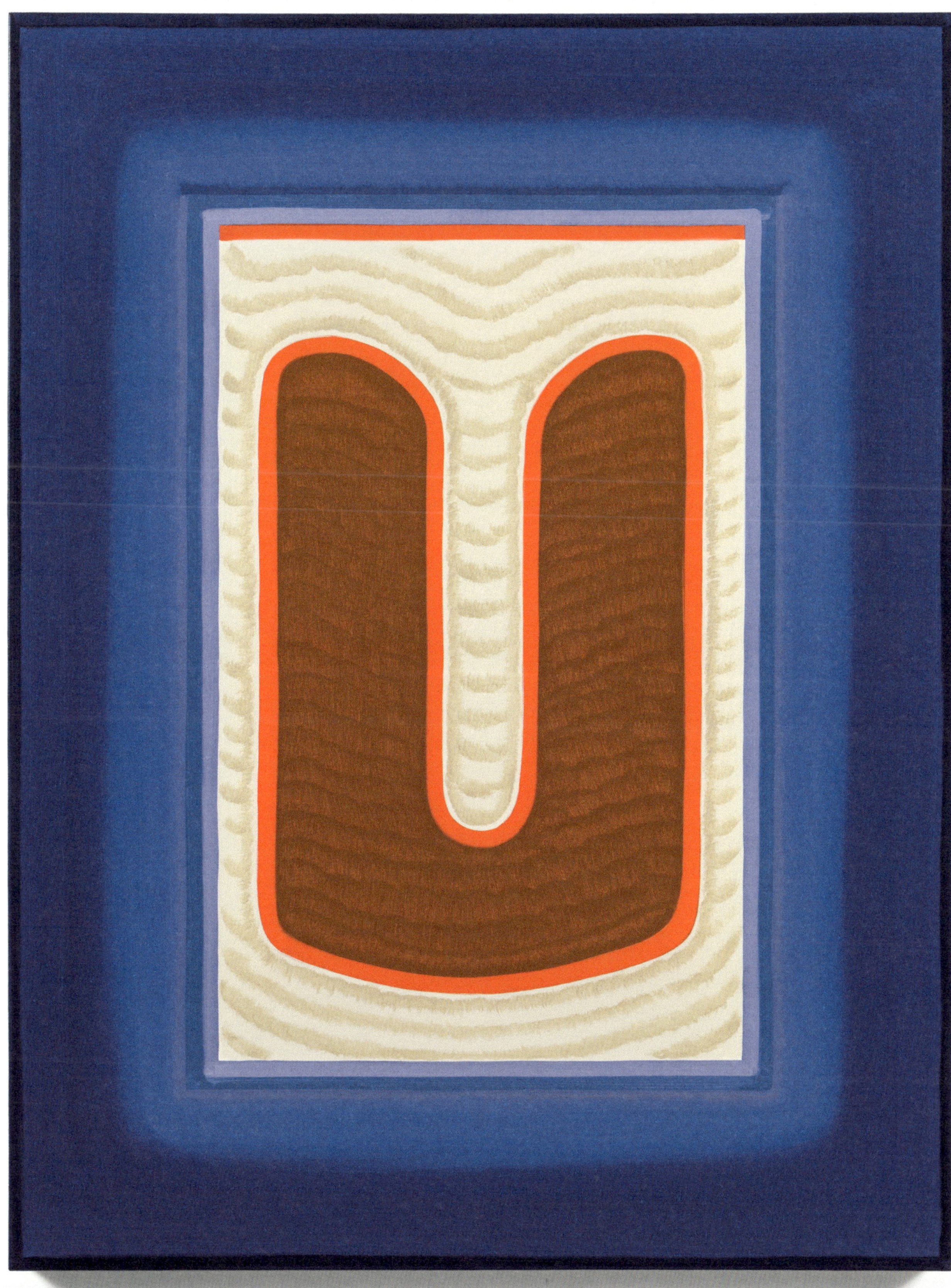

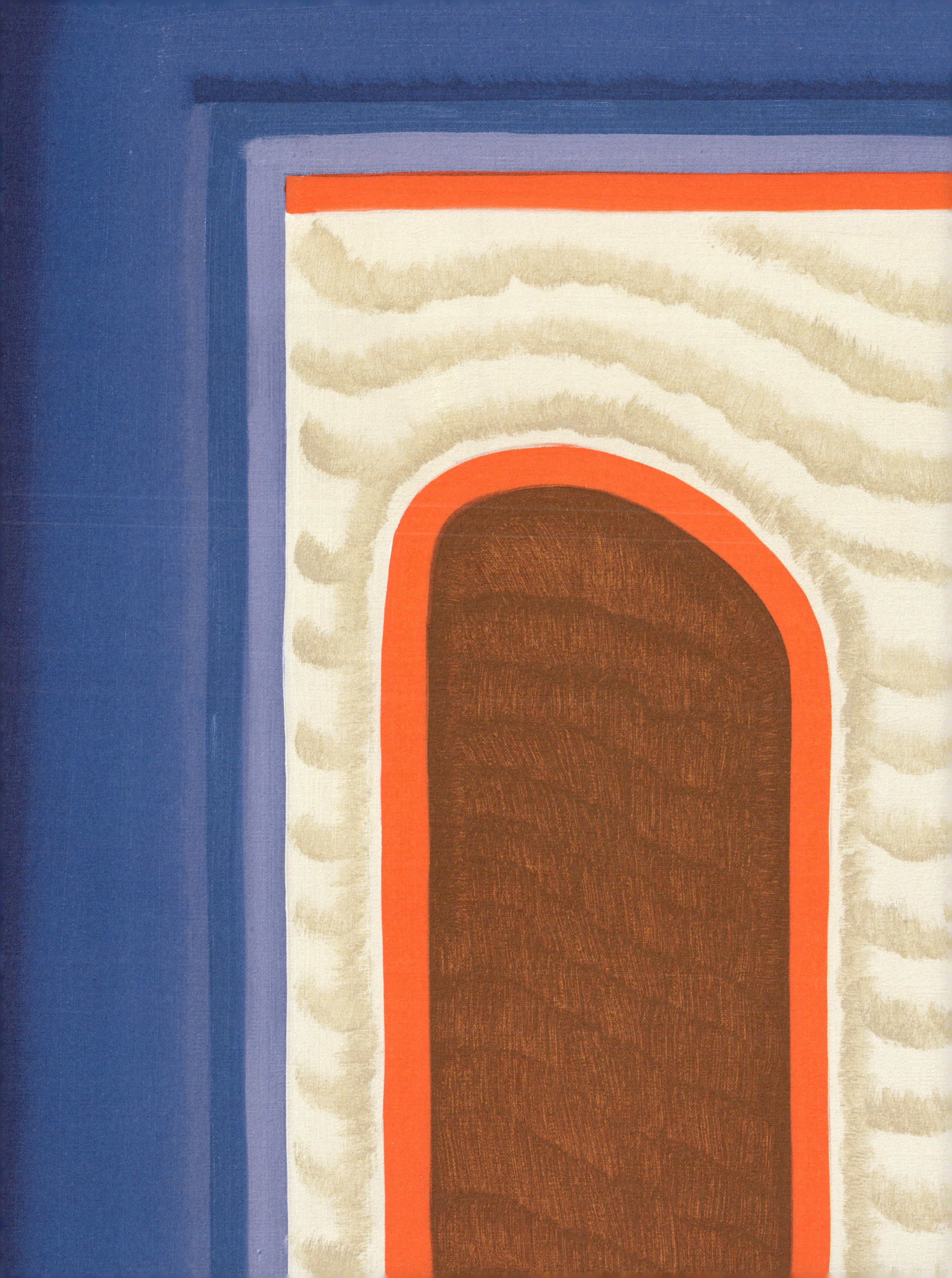

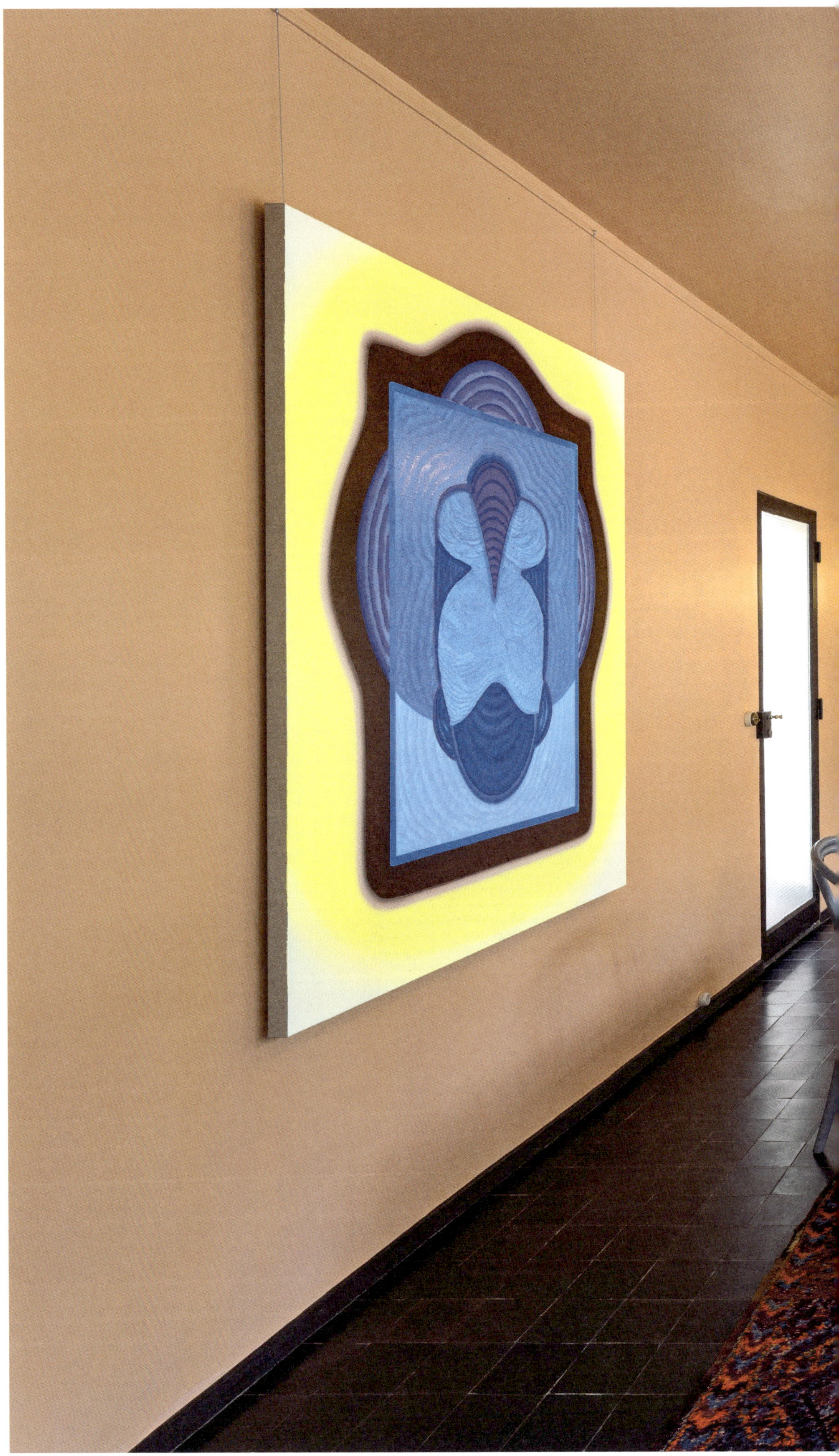

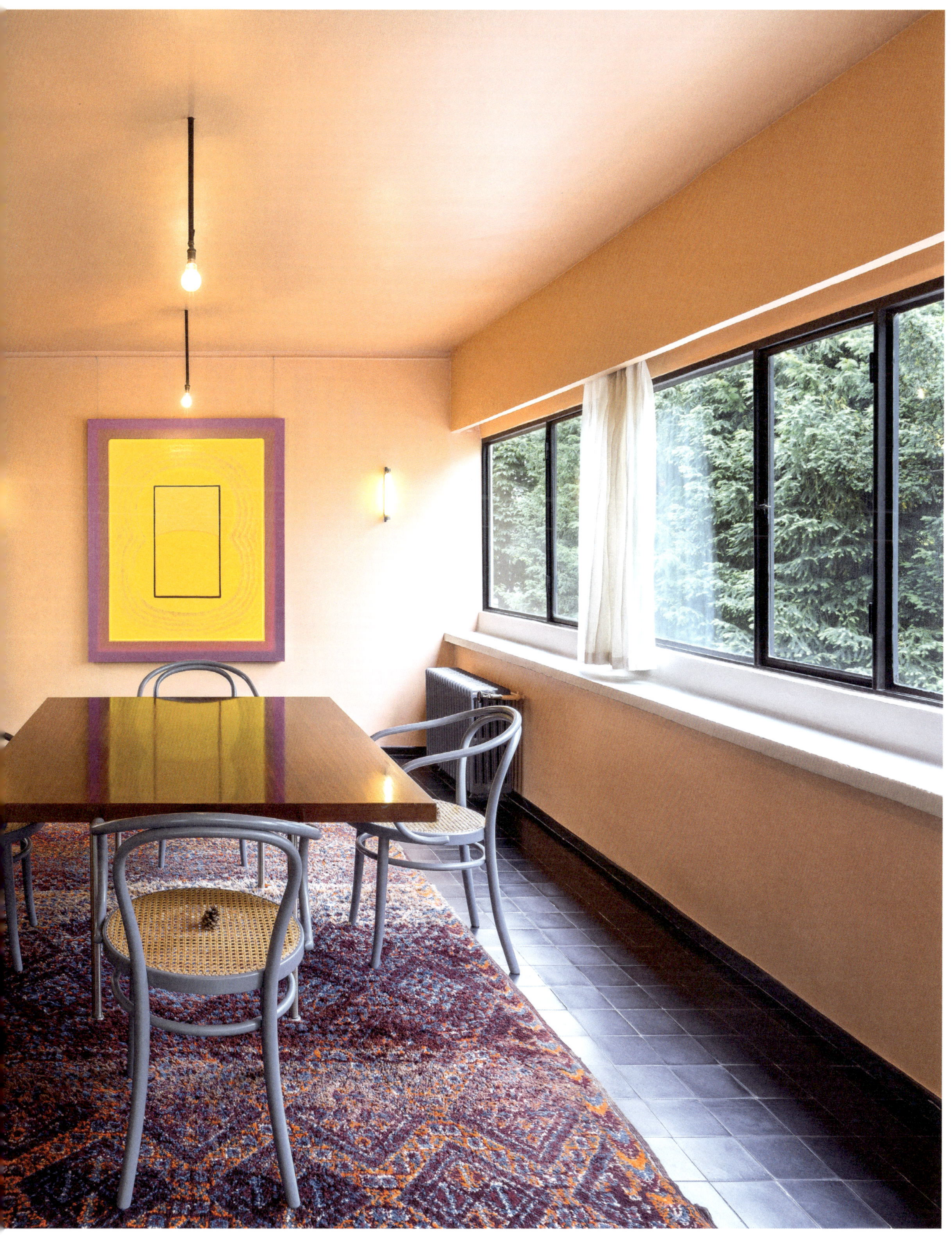

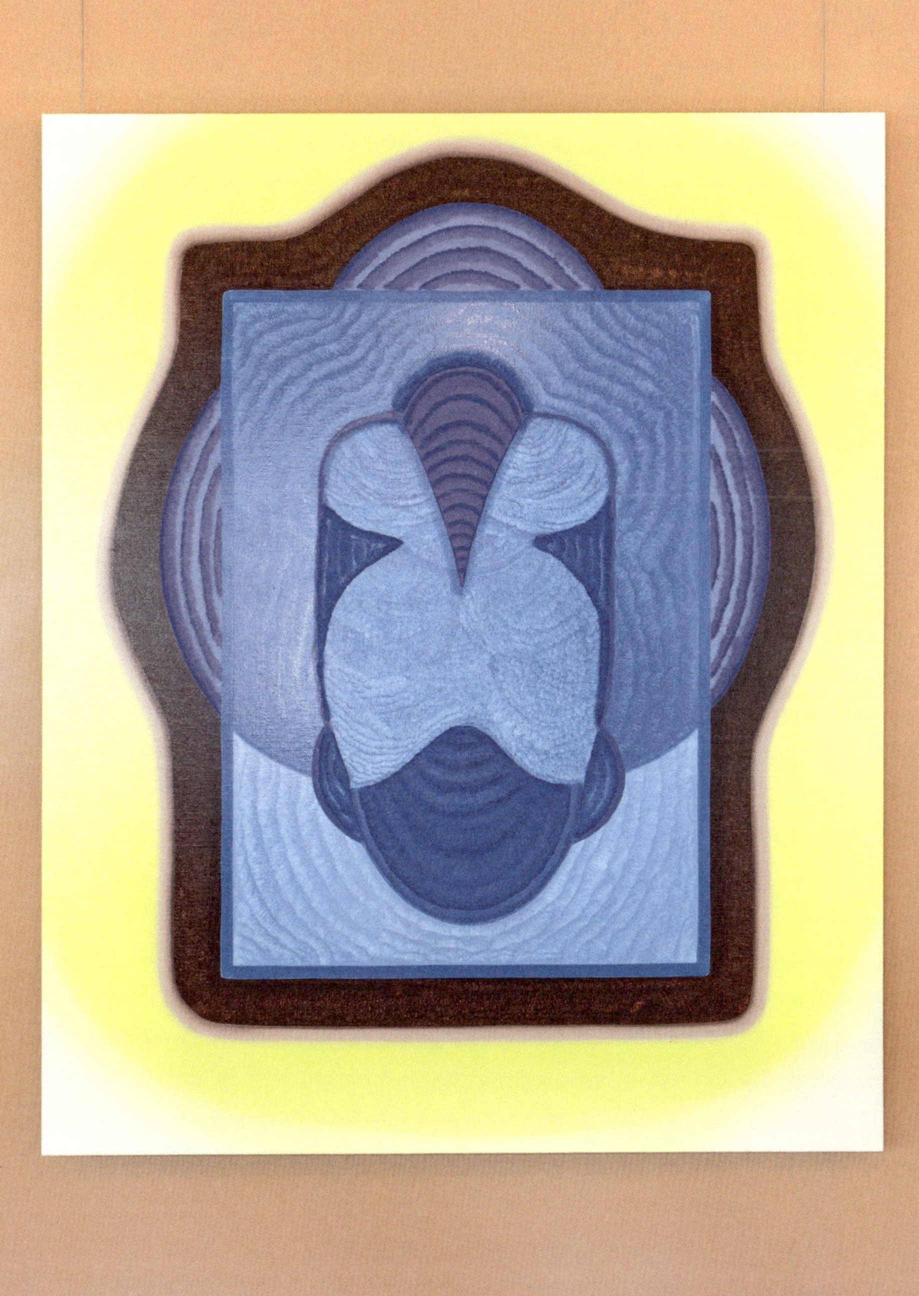

June Morning, oil on linen, 100 × 73 × 2.5 cm (62 × 50 inches)

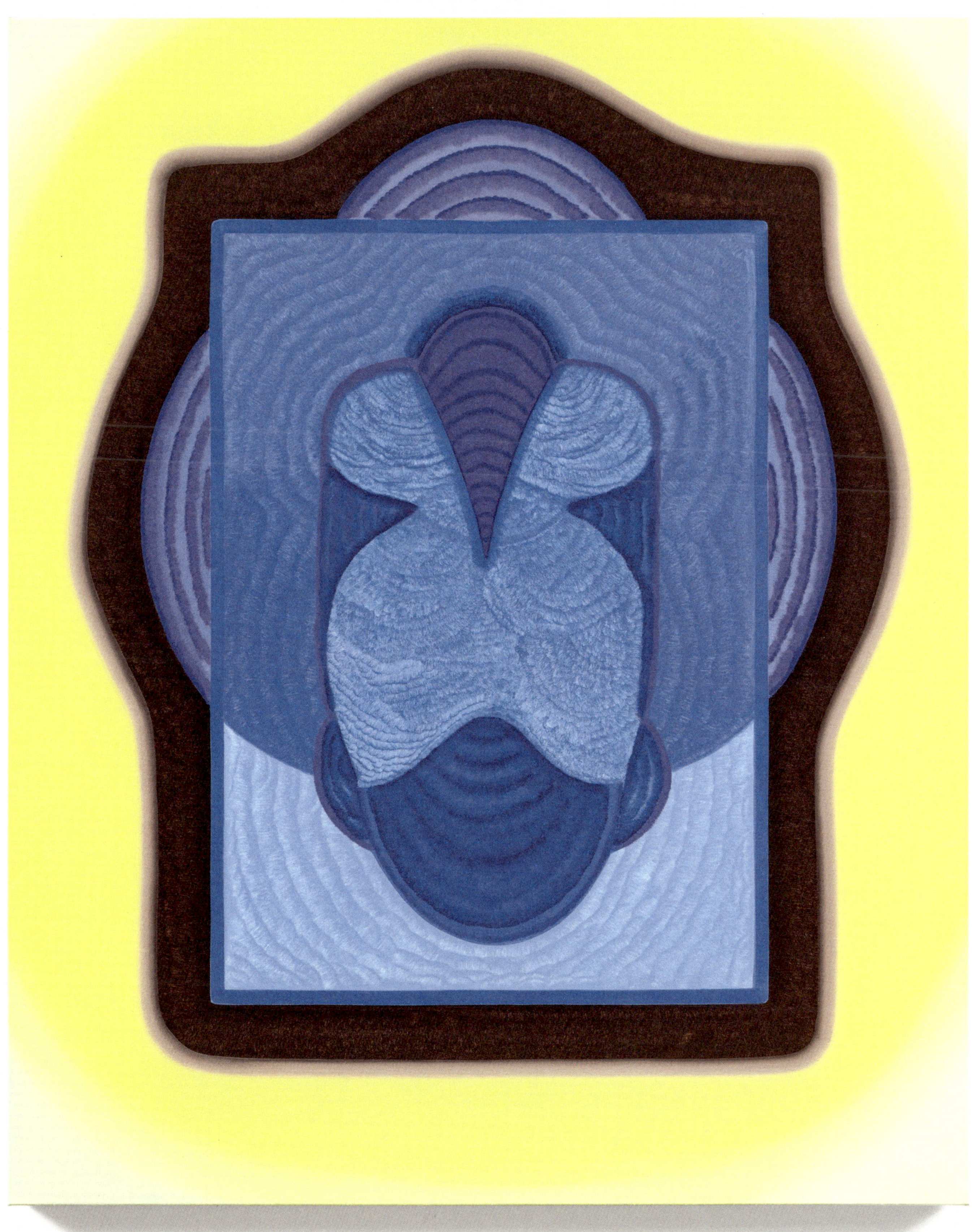

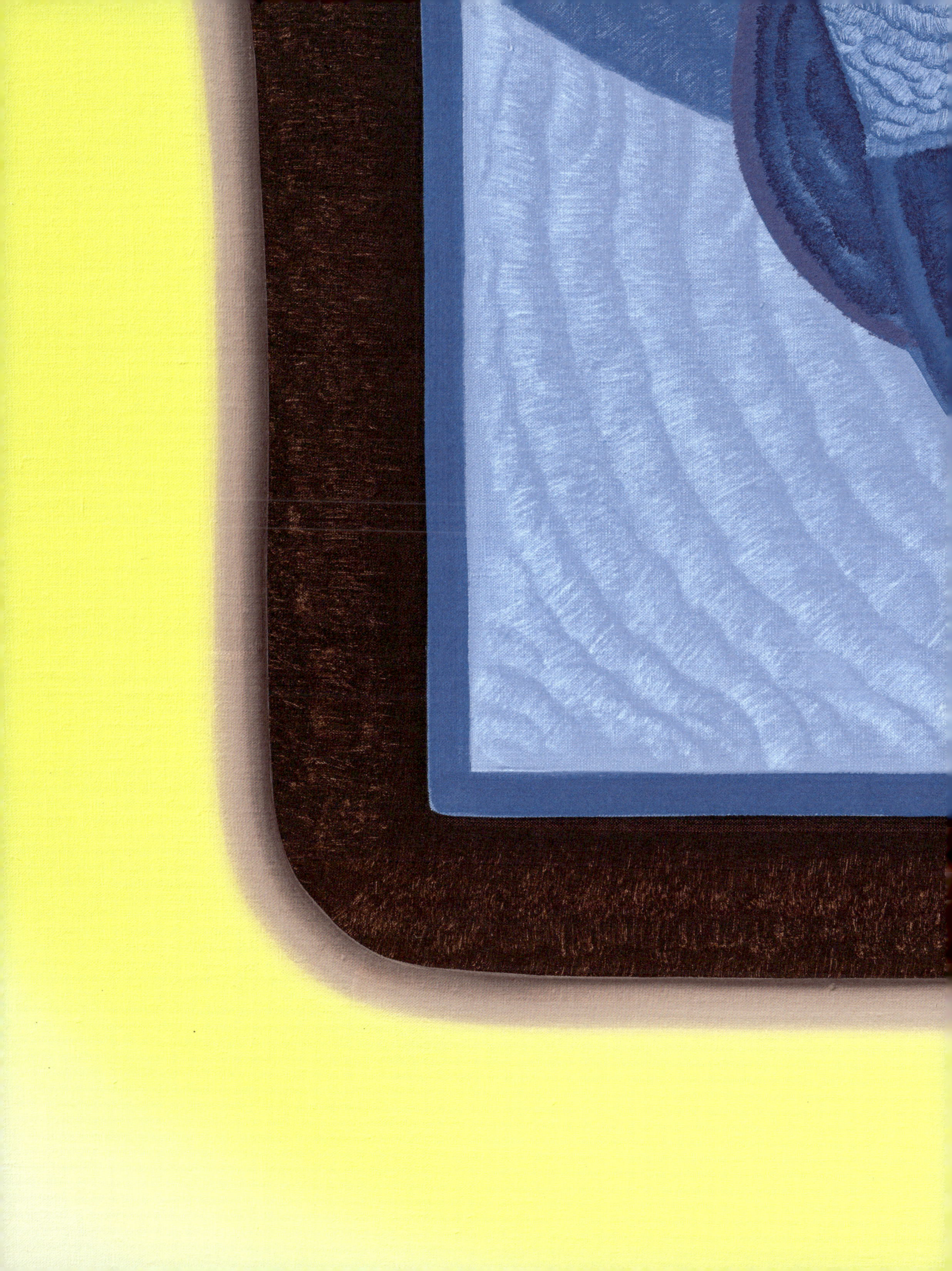

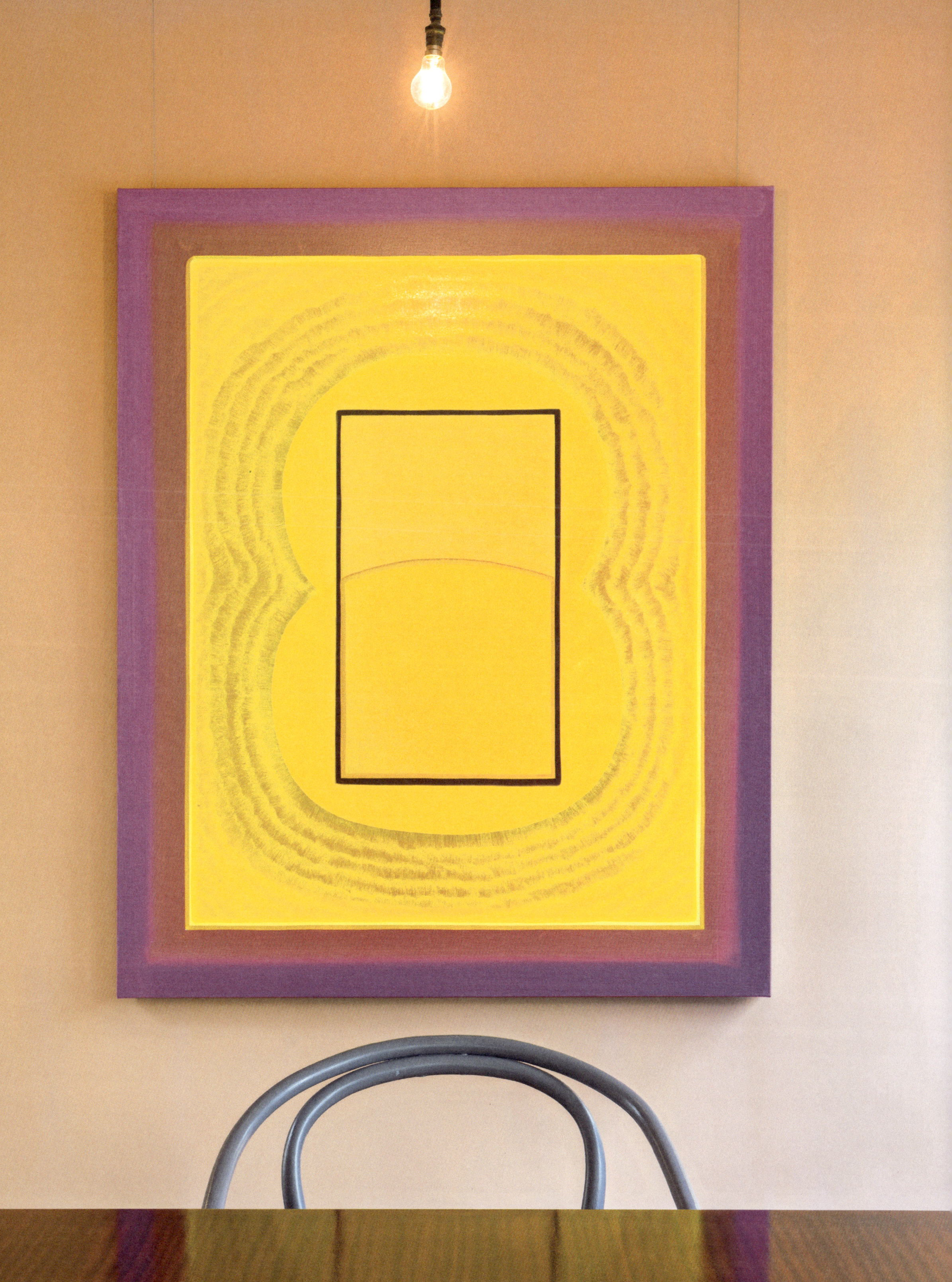

Apollinaire, oil on linen, 100 × 73 × 2.5 cm (62 × 50 inches)

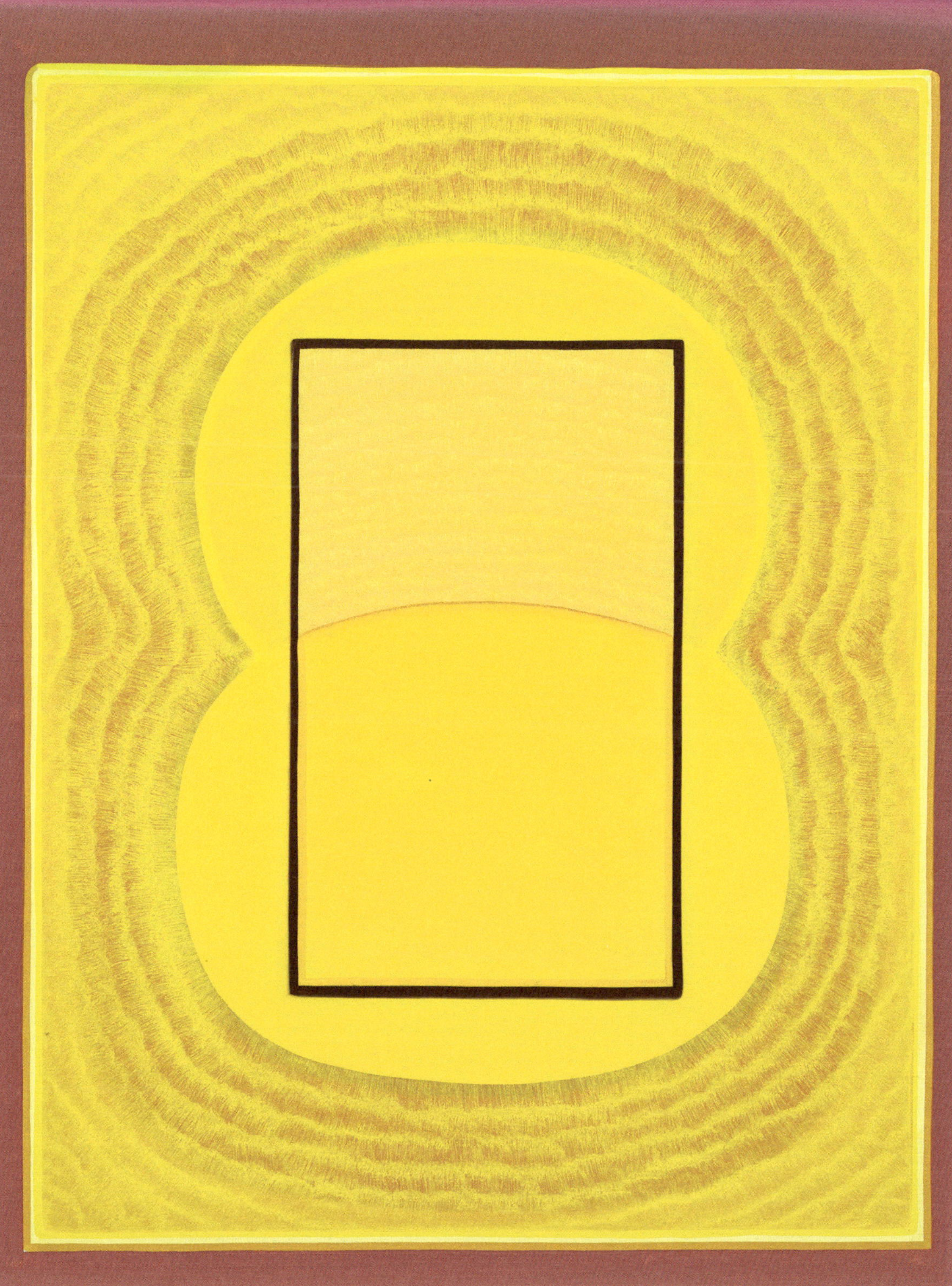

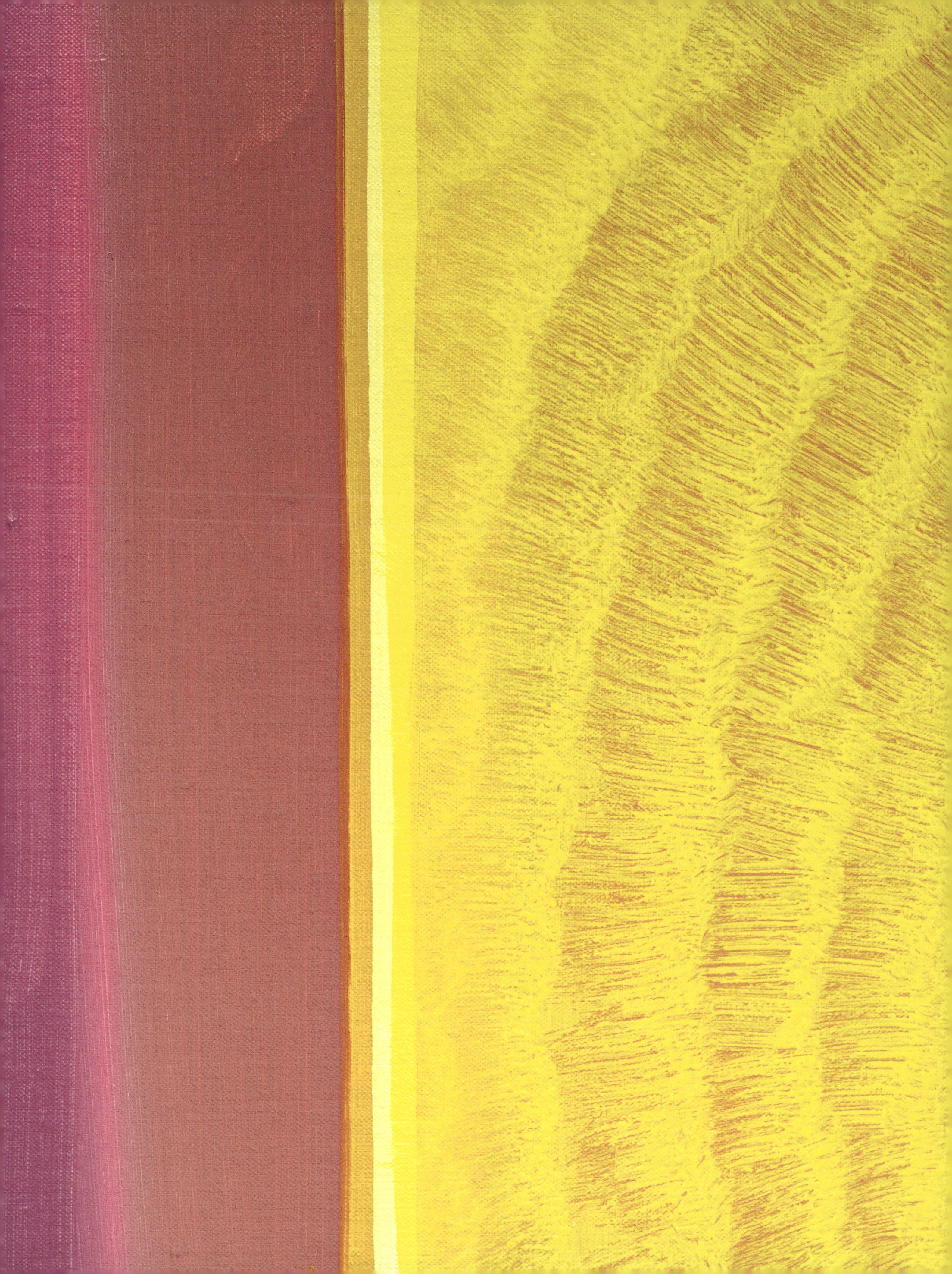

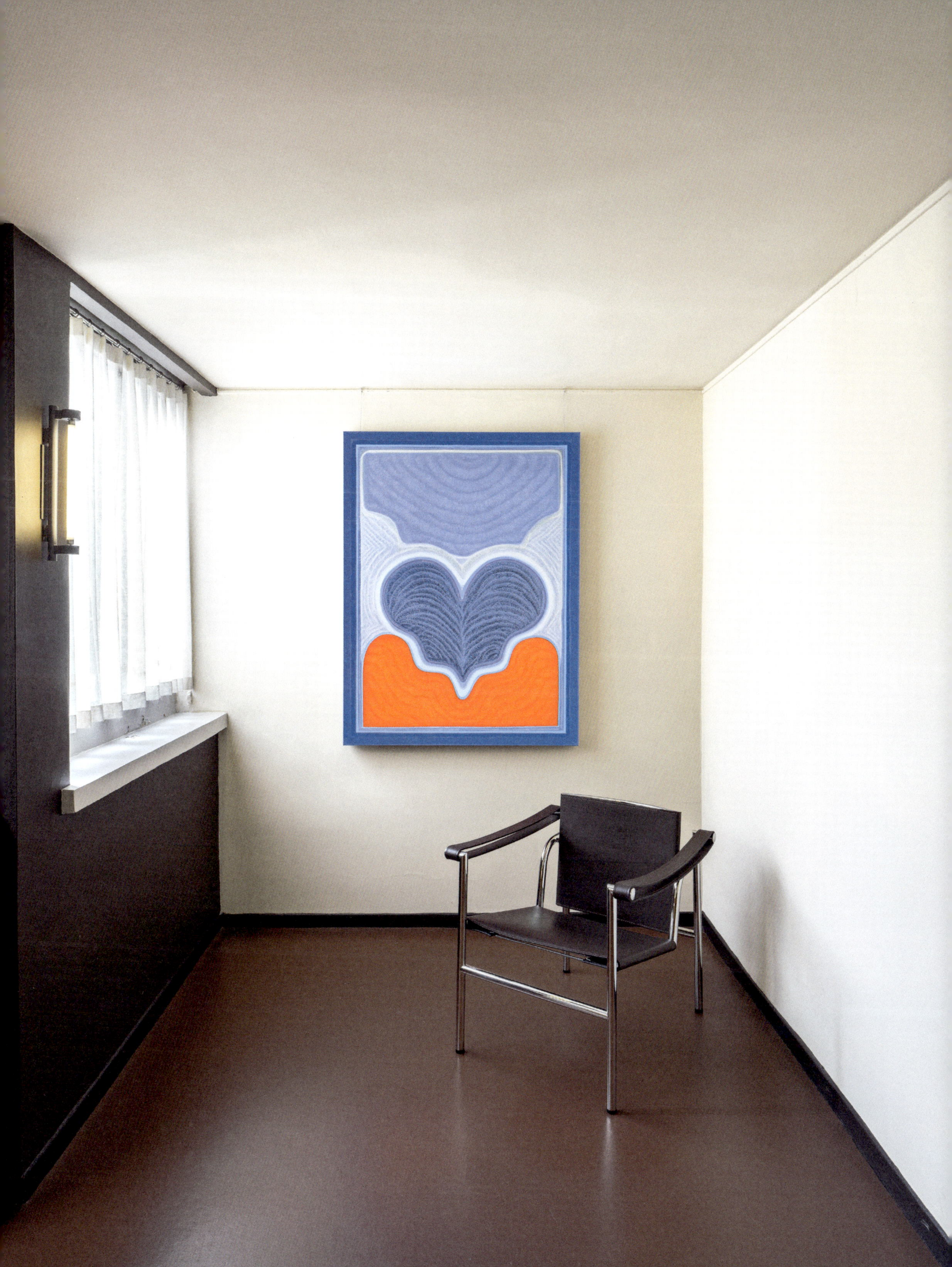

Clouds Over Vétheuil, oil on linen, 100 × 73 × 2.5 cm (48 × 36 inches)

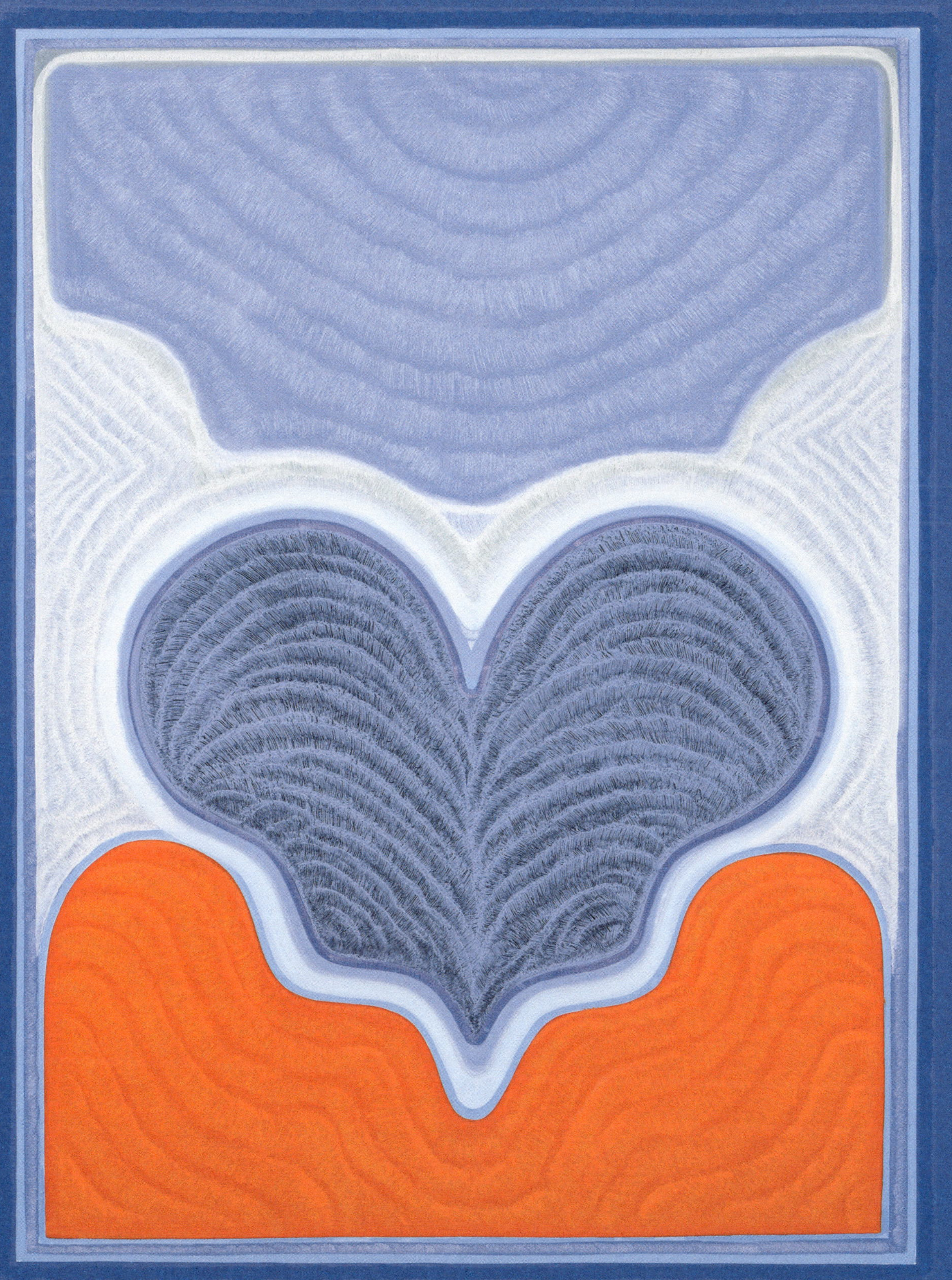

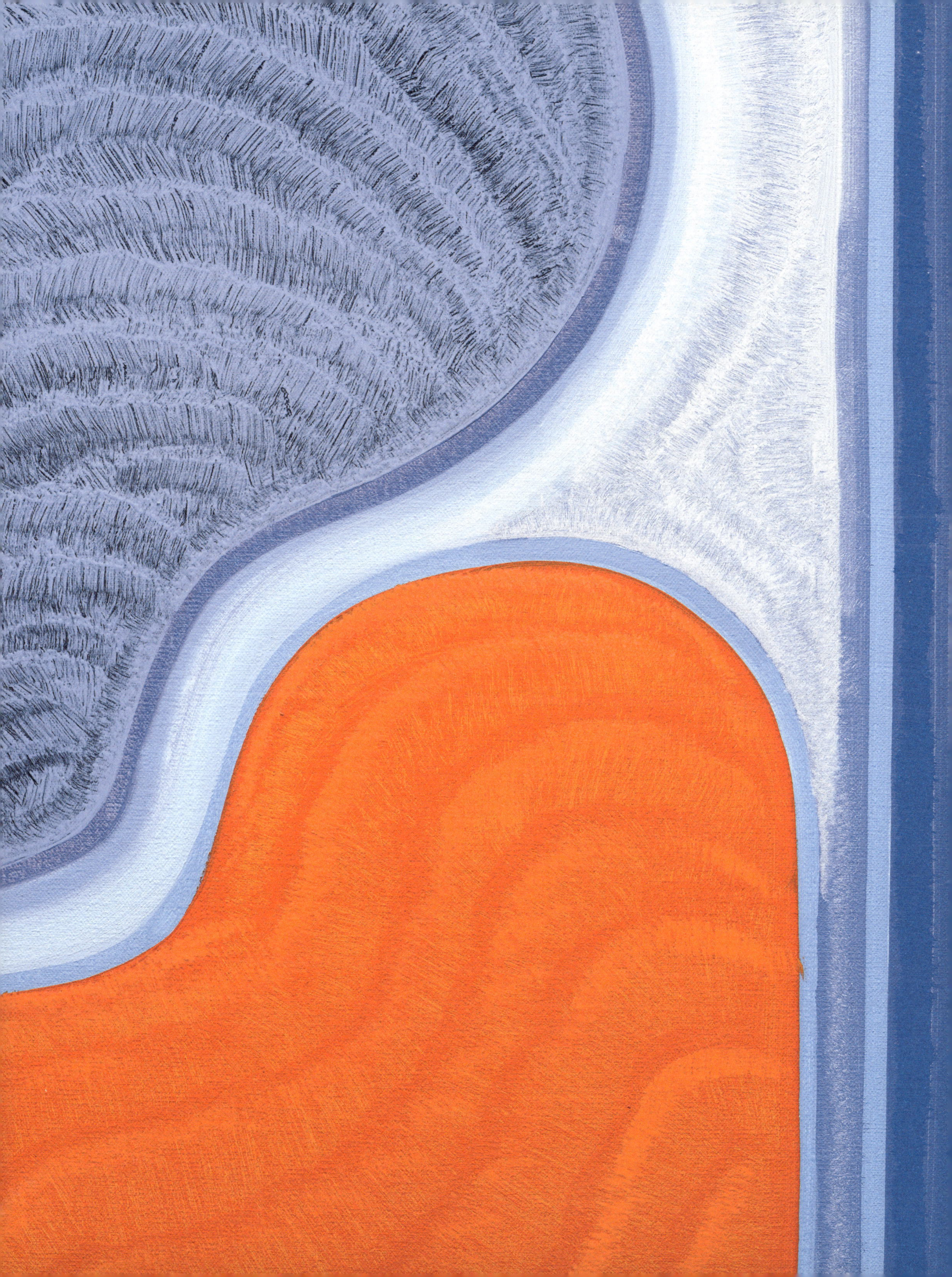

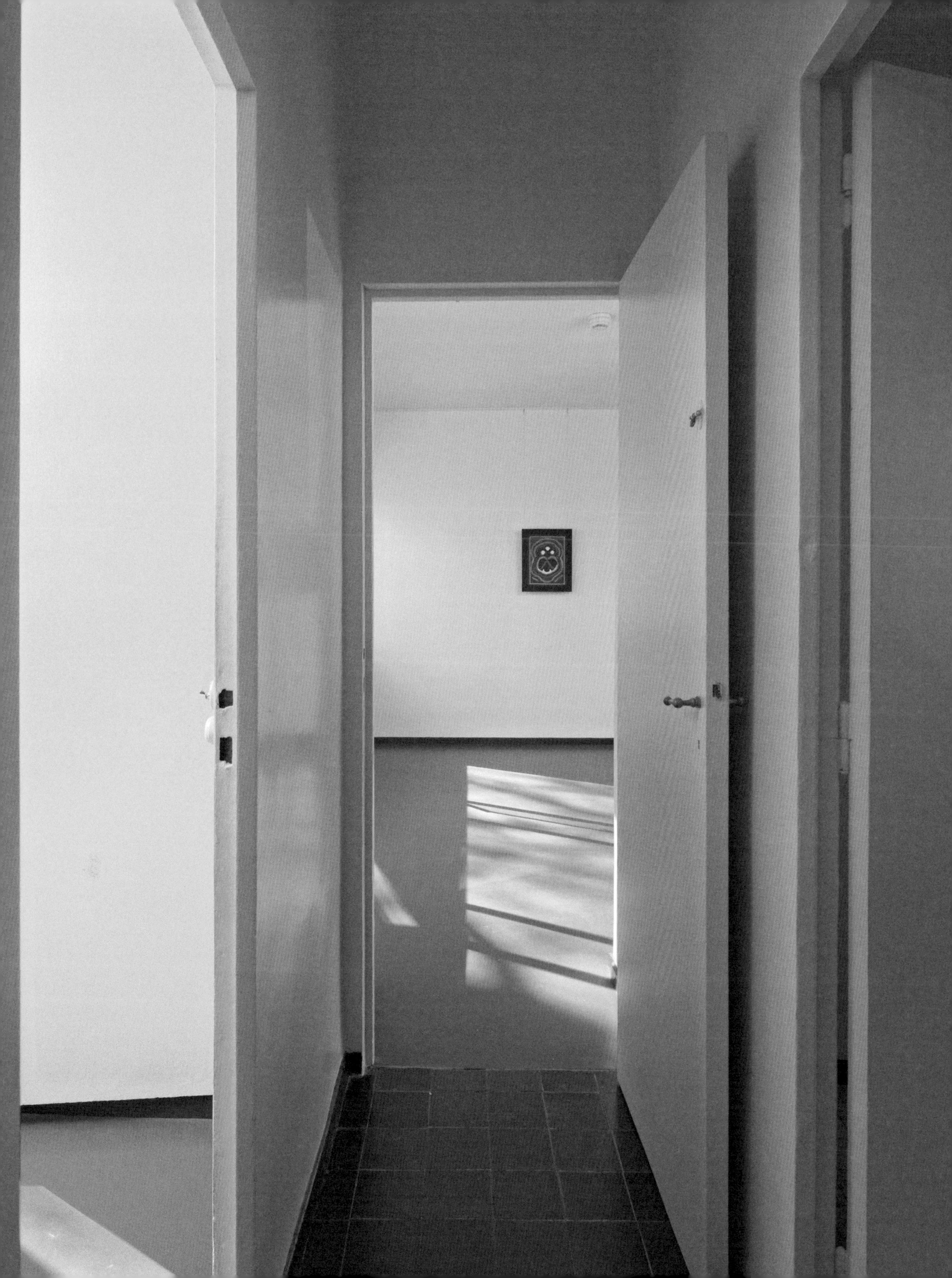

Black Pansy, oil on linen, 100 × 73 × 2.5 cm (20 × 16 inches)

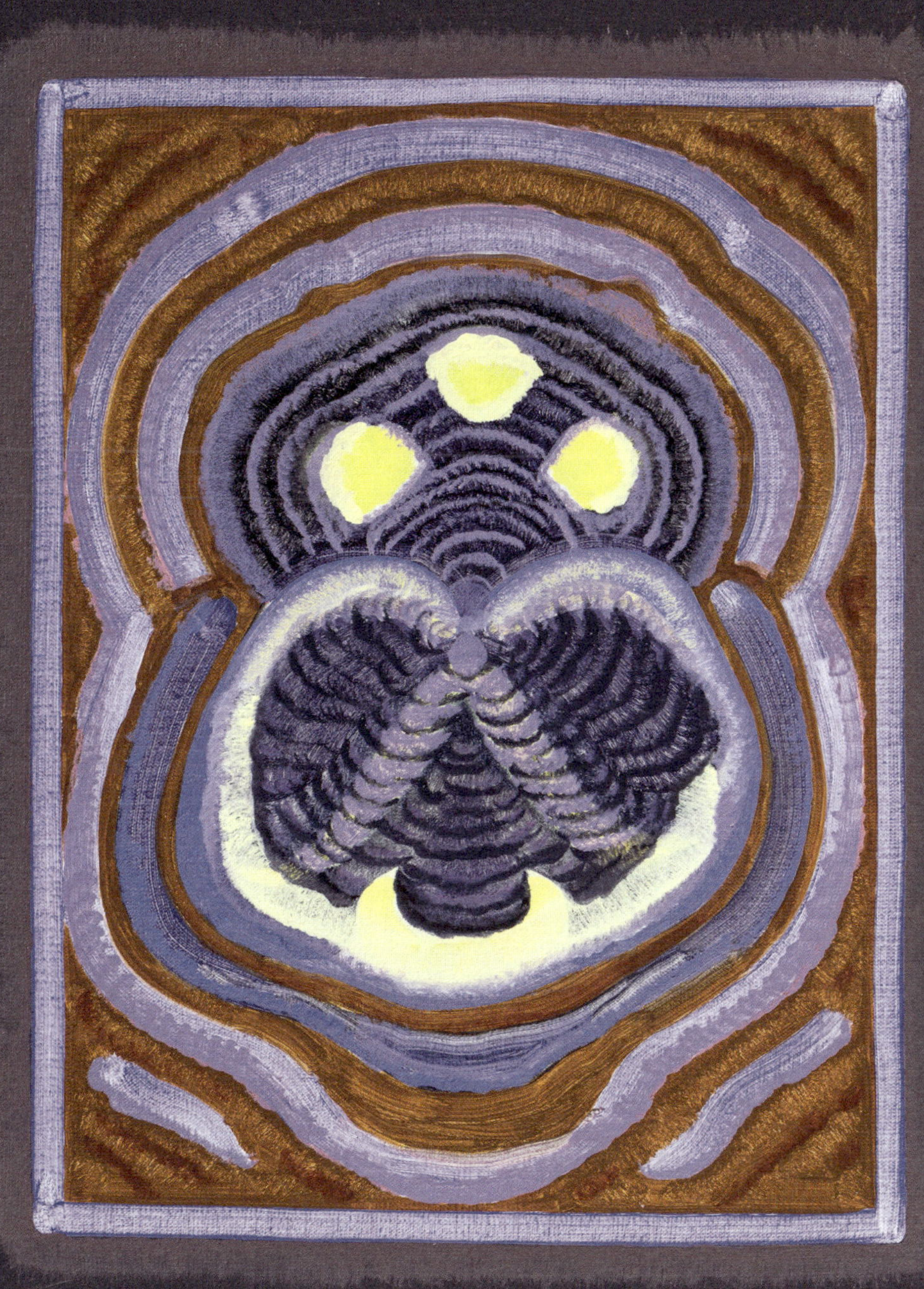

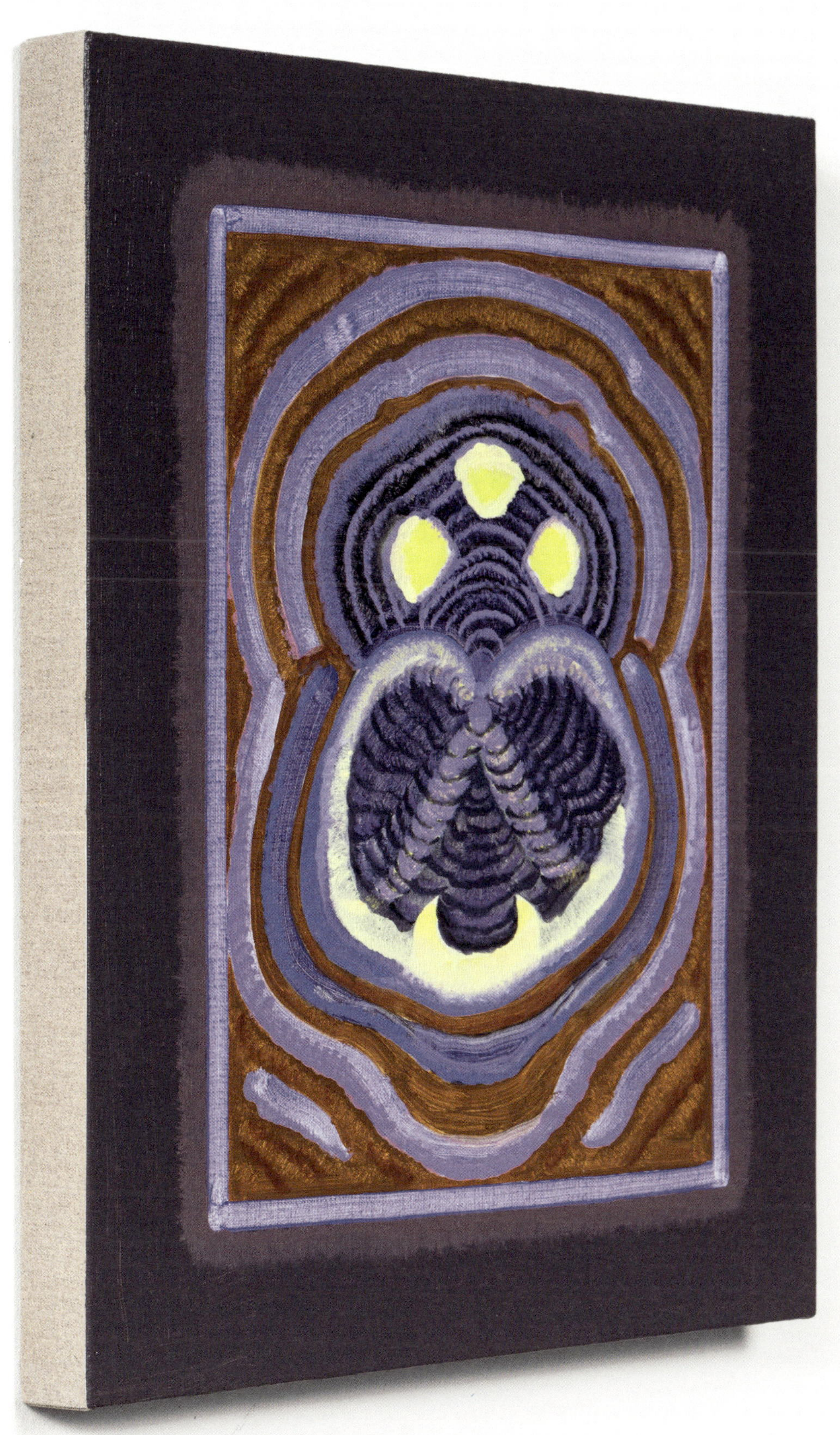

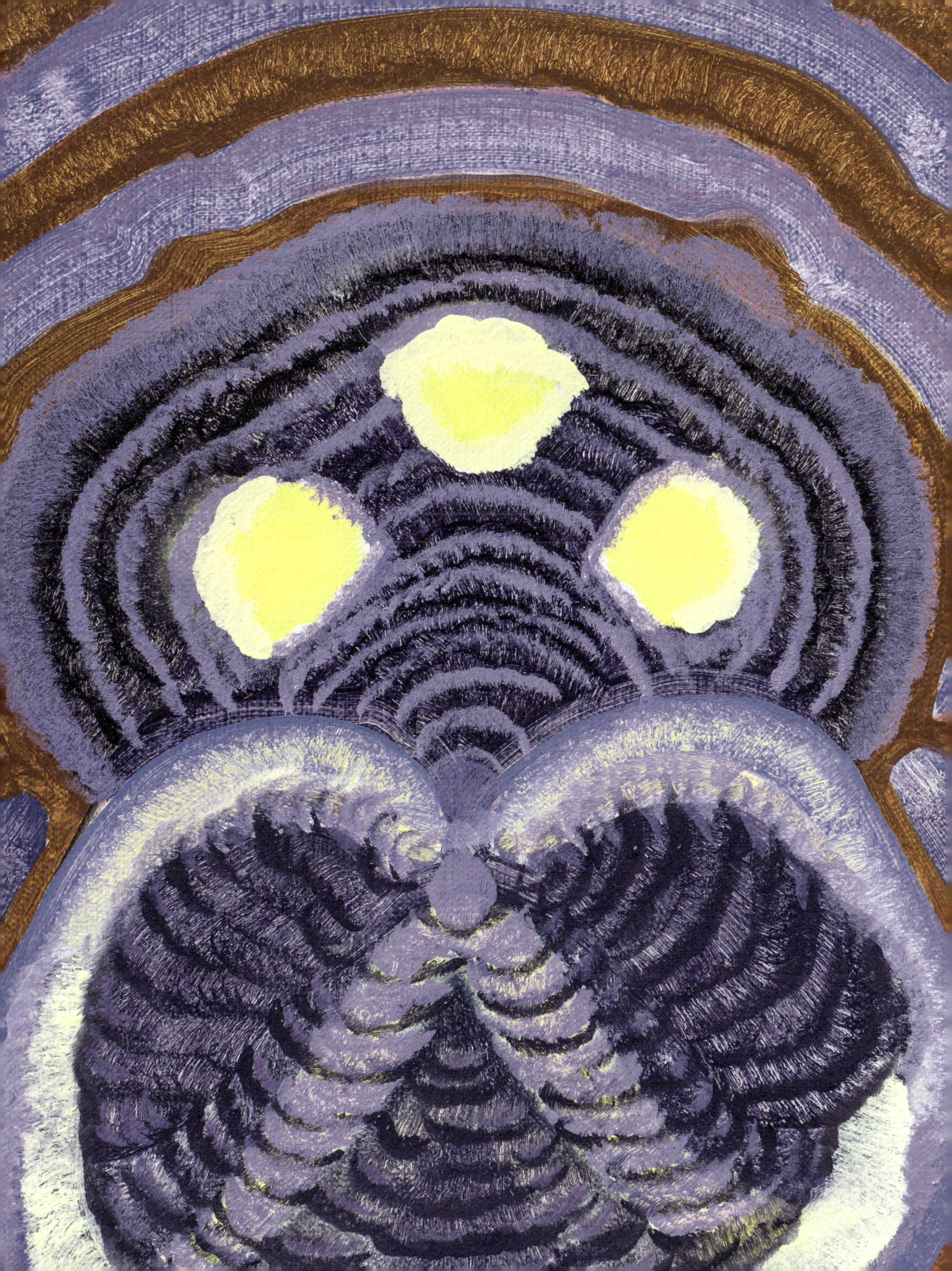

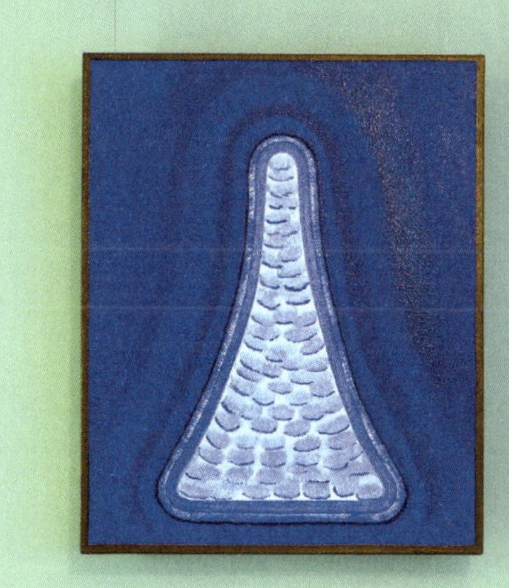

Blue Corydalis, oil on linen, 100 × 73 × 2.5 cm (20 × 16 inches)

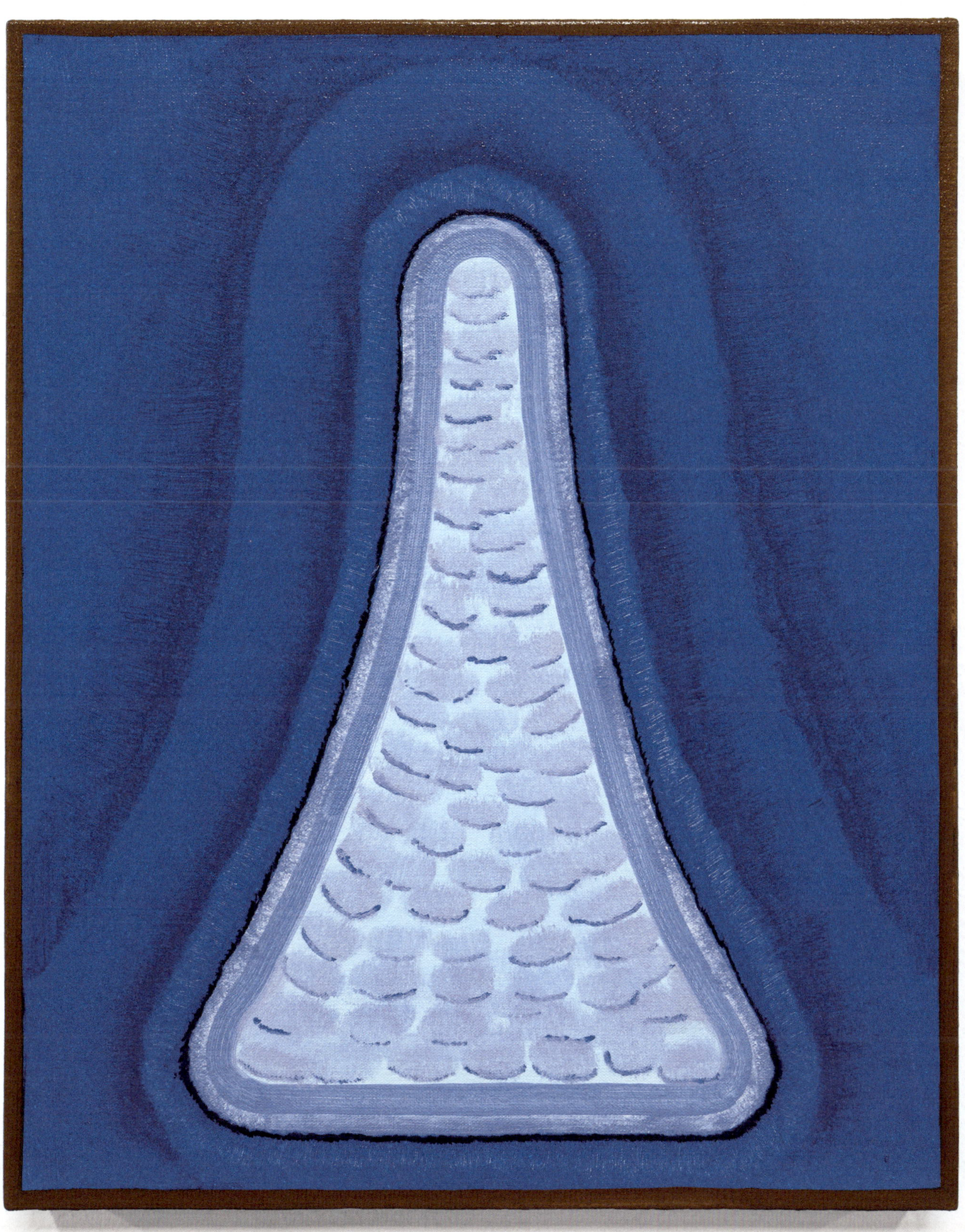

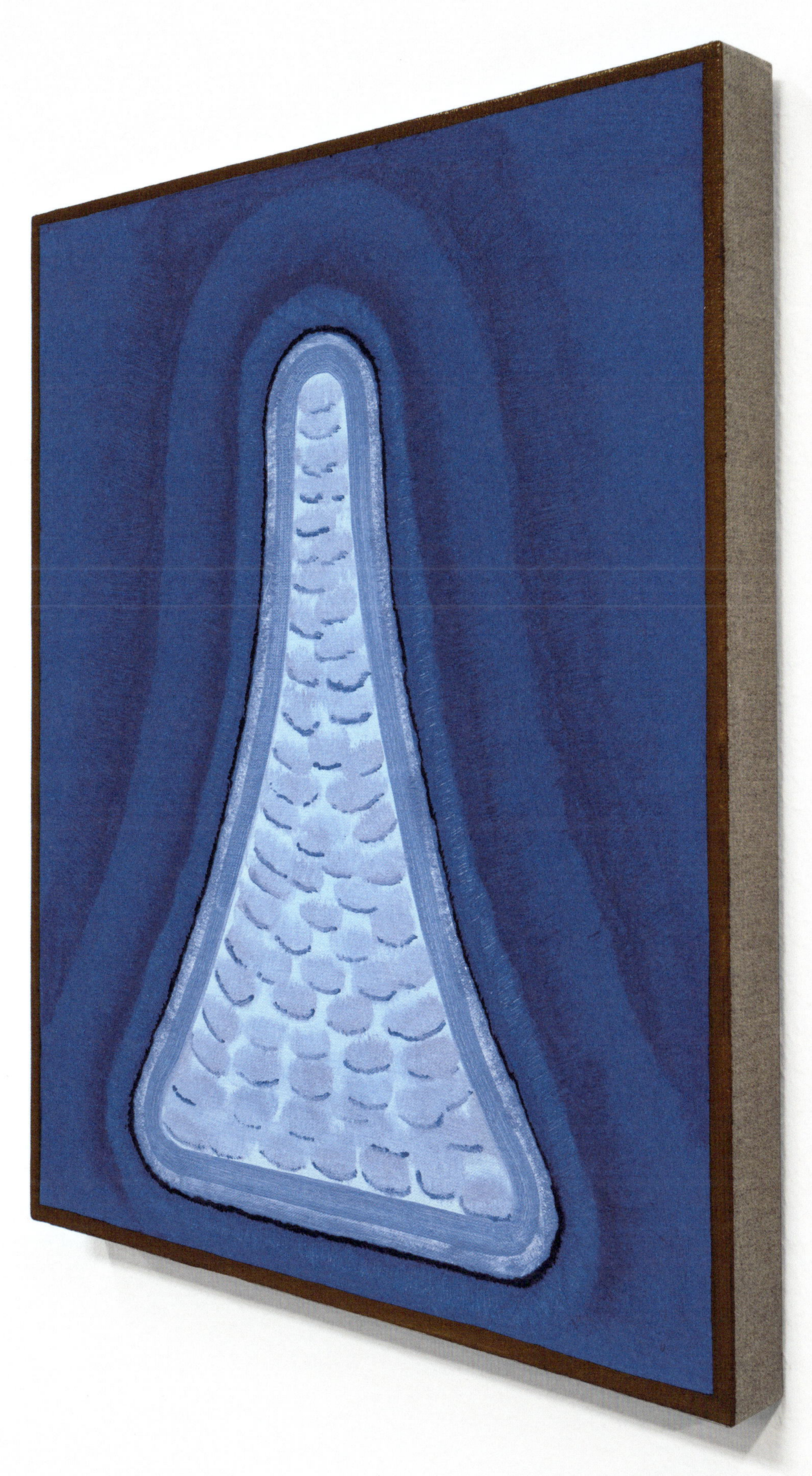

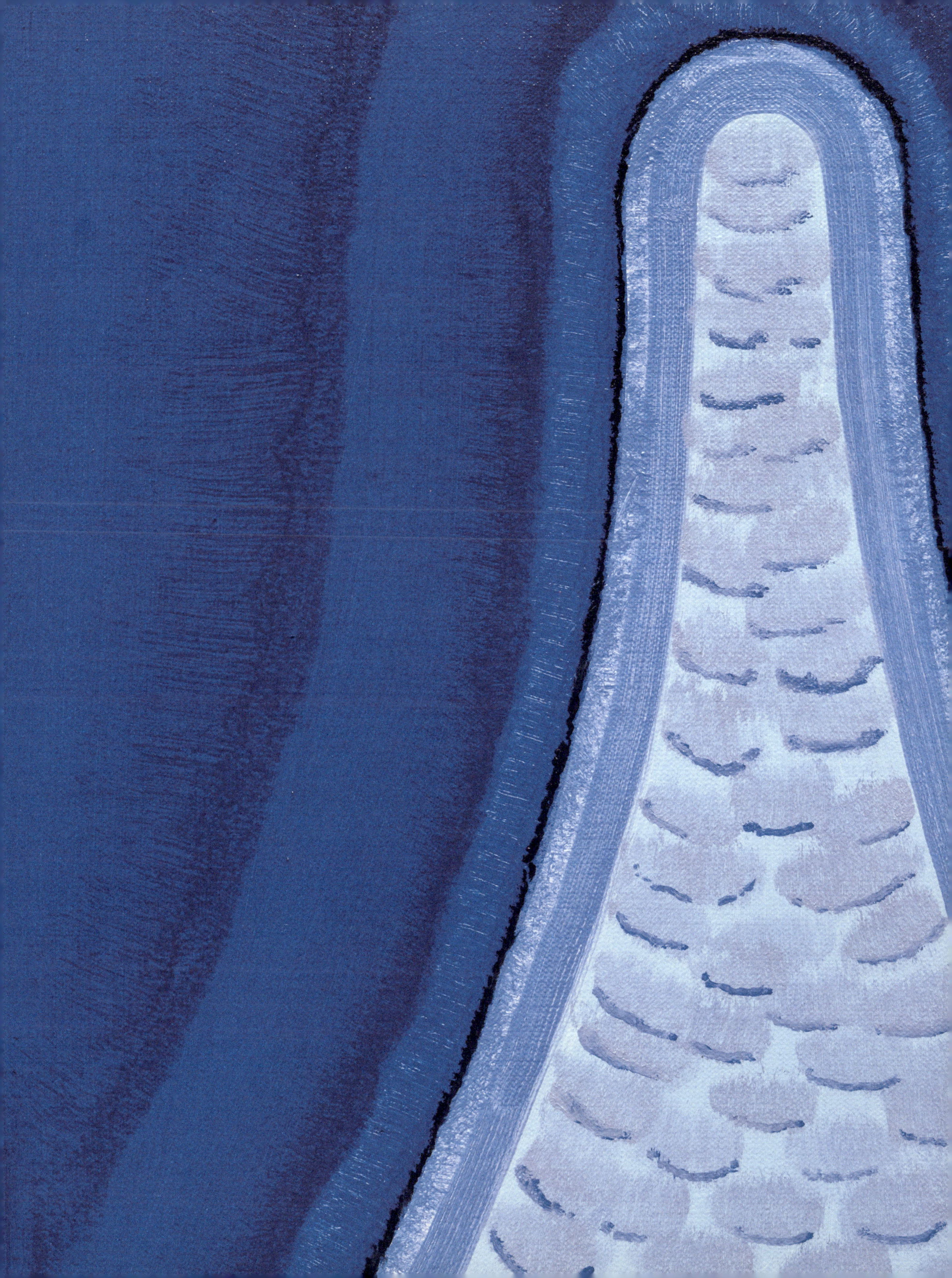

CONTROL THE LIGHT: LILY STOCKMAN'S PAINTINGS AT MAISON LA ROCHE

Jennifer Higgie

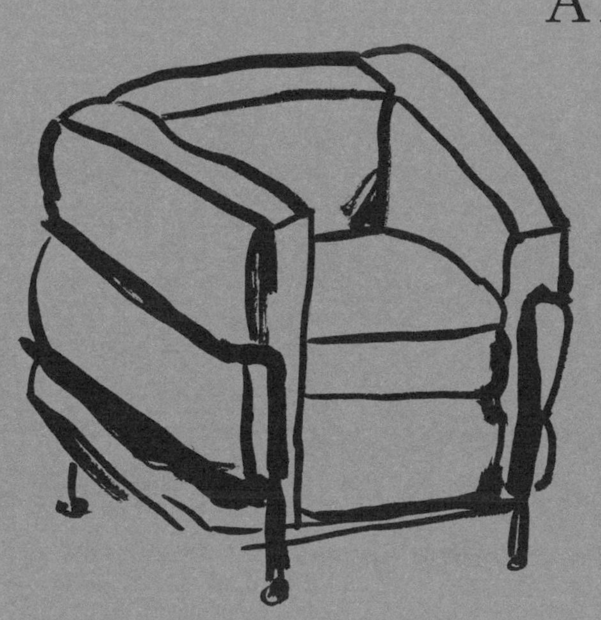

All drawings by Lily Stockman

Like ancient symbols reimagined and flung into the future, throughout the light-filled minimalism of Maison La Roche, Lily Stockman's eleven paintings hum and pulsate with vivid colors, chromatic harmonies, and enigmatic forms that animate the building's sleek walls and polished surfaces. Stockman, who is "interested in buoyancy," describes her compositions as "contained oceans." "Everything," she says, "floats at a different frequency."[1]

Maison La Roche and the nextdoor Maison Jeanneret were designed and built in Paris's 16th Arrondissement between 1923 and 1925 by the artist and architect Le Corbusier and his cousin, the architect Pierre Jeanneret. This complex comprises two buildings: a home for Le Corbusier's brother, Albert Jeanneret, and his wife, Lotti Rääf, and their children, and an apartment "intended for an unmarried man, the owner of a modern painting collection with a passion for art."[2] The man in question, Raoul La Roche, collected works by Le Corbusier, Juan Gris, Fernand Léger, Amédée Ozenfant, Pablo Picasso, and others—artists to whom myths and motifs of the deep past were as thrilling as the invention of new languages for a new world.

The use of modern building materials such as reinforced concrete allowed Le Corbusier the freedom to realize what he termed his "five points of a new architecture": the free facade, free plan, long windows, garden roof, and pilotis (a grid of delicate concrete pylons that support the weight of the building). He designed the ramp, which is a central feature of the building, so as to avoid what Stockman describes as "the percussive step of the body on stairs"; "the idea of floating between the elevations was more poetic to him." But the architect was interested in more than structural challenges; a lifelong painter, he was fascinated with how color might combine with architecture, and he painted the walls and ceilings in variations of dark gray, ultramarine blue, Paris green, sienna earth, burnt umber, ivory, and black.[3] When she was offered the opportunity to stage an exhibition in this unique building, Stockman decided to respond to the architecture using colors dictated by Le Corbusier's palette—an approach to repetition and renewal the Swiss architect would surely have appreciated.

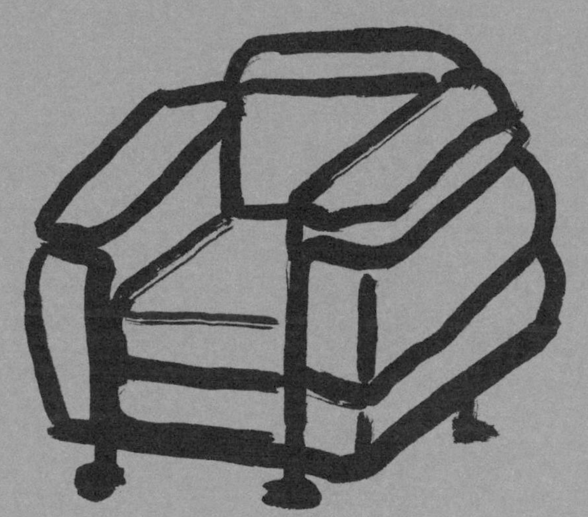

The seed of Stockman's interest in Le Corbusier's work was planted in her student years. She learned to paint in the Carpenter Center for the Visual Arts at Harvard University, the only building that he designed

1 Unless otherwise indicated, all artist quotes come from a Zoom conversation with the author on May 7, 2024.

2 "Maisons La Roche et Jeanneret, Paris, France, 1923–1925," Fondation Le Corbusier, https://www.fondationlecorbusier.fr/en/work-architecture/achievements-maisons-la-roche-jeanneret-pais-france-1923-1925/.

3 "The Question of Colour," Fondation Le Corbusier, http://www.fondationlecorbusier.fr/wp-content/uploads/2022/05/2049_5522.pdf.

4
Pablo Picasso,
Minotaur Ravishing a Female Centaur,
1933, Museum of Modern Art, New York, https://www.moma.org/collection/works/64803.

(with the collaboration of Chilean architect Guillermo Jullian de la Fuente) in North America. In winter, she and her fellow students liked to slide down its ramp on metal trays pilfered from the canteen. The artist describes it as "a big, marvelous, Brutalist, imposing kind of building" that one architecture critic disparagingly described as resembling "mating pianos." The painting atelier is on the third floor, Stockman says, and features "dozens of these very tall, slender windows with individual cadmium-yellow louvers that you can open and close to control the light. There is this kind of spaceship-like skylight and an open floor plan, with a huge, six-bay soapstone sink, with generations of paint daubs all over it."

Stockman believes that working in Le Corbusier's building taught her how to paint, how to think about light and volume, and "how to move through space." ("Space," he famously said, "is the breath of art.") After she graduated, the young artist studied miniature painting in Jaipur, India, and *thangka* painting (sacred scrolls that combine depictions of Buddhist deities, mandalas, and events of spiritual significance) in Mongolia. She also traveled to Chandigarh, the northern Indian "city of the future" and Punjab's new state capital, which Le Corbusier worked on from 1950 until 1965, alongside a team of architects and urban planners. It's clearly a city that emerged from a painter's vision: the High Court, for instance, includes a soaring bright-yellow column flanked by slabs of red and green walls, like an abstract painting come to life.

Invited to create new works for Maison La Roche, Stockman did a deep dive into Le Corbusier's buildings, but also into his journals, sketches, paintings, and collages. Eventually she arrived upon the ancient Greek story of the Minotaur as a unifying theme. A monstrous half-man, half-bull who was imprisoned by King Minos in a labyrinth beneath the palace at Knossos in Crete, the Minotaur was eventually slain by the hero Theseus, who was aided by his lover, Ariadne, the Minotaur's half-sister. In India, as we know, cows are sacred, and coexist with people on the city streets. It was when he began work in Chandigarh that Le Corbusier started painting images of, and writing poetry about, bulls entwined with humans, often rendering their noses and eyes as symbols of infinity. The Surrealists, too, were fascinated by the Minotaur, believing it the "personification of forbidden desires,"[4] which is why they titled their magazine after it. Both Le Corbusier and Picasso repeatedly drew and painted the Minotaur, attracted not only by its potent mix of masculinity and despair, vulnerability and irrationality, but also by the fact that it is an ancient story with great contemporary relevance: in Jungian psychology, the labyrinth is understood as a reflection of

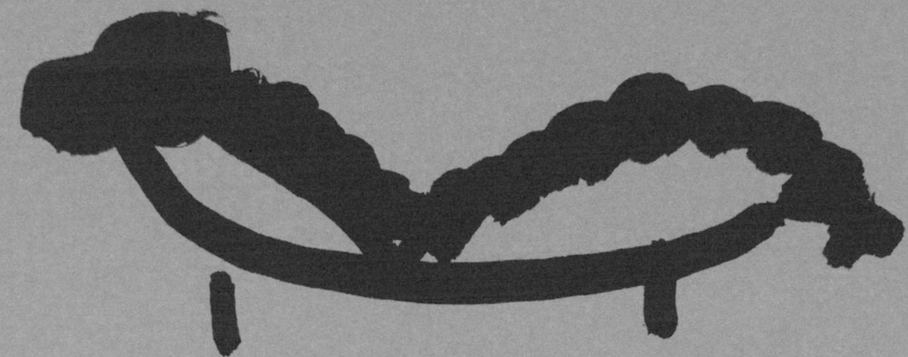

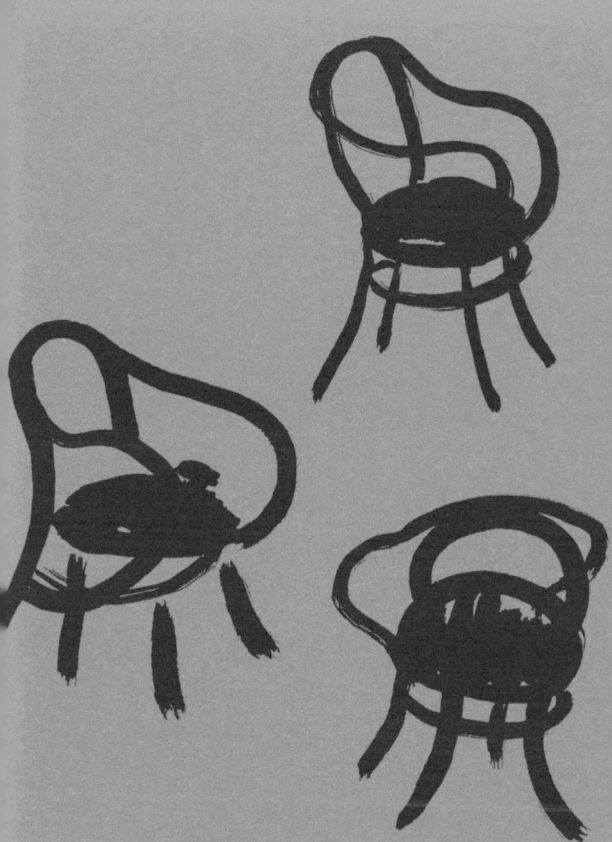

the complexities of the human psyche and the Minotaur a symbol of the "shadow"—the unconscious part of each person's personality that harbors repressed thoughts and desires.

As the first woman artist from the United States to exhibit in Maison La Roche—a building designed by a man—and as someone who, in her own words, was "wending her way through the labyrinth of life experience," Stockman decided to appropriate this most masculine of motifs and reconfigure it through a female lens. Wanting to "haunt" the building's past and "take the head of the bull and plonk it on my own shoulders while I wandered through that space," she created hand-painted geometries whose dreamy symbolism and organic individuality counter the slick modernity of the building's design, even as they honor its light and space. The Minotaur's influence is manifest not via an evocation of the creature's physical form, but in a sense of vitality, intense feeling, and searching.

Each of Stockman's paintings evolves from an intertwining of influences, instinct, feeling, and invention. The rhythmic purple of *Metronome* (all works 2024), for example, was inspired by the textiles the artist first saw in Jaipur and Chandigarh. Its title alludes not only to the instrument musicians use to keep time, but also to the precision with which Stockman placed the picture within the building so the afternoon light would hit its surface, illuminating its intensities and "allowing the energy to flow up and out of the composition."[5] By contrast, *Chandigarh*—a hot orange, textured shape like a swelling thumb and its echo, outlined by a soft lilac moat—alludes to Le Corbusier's *Open Hand Monument*, posthumously erected in Chandigarh in 1985. A twenty-six-meter-high sculpture that rotates in the wind, it symbolizes "the hand to give and the hand to take; peace and prosperity, and the unity of mankind."[6]

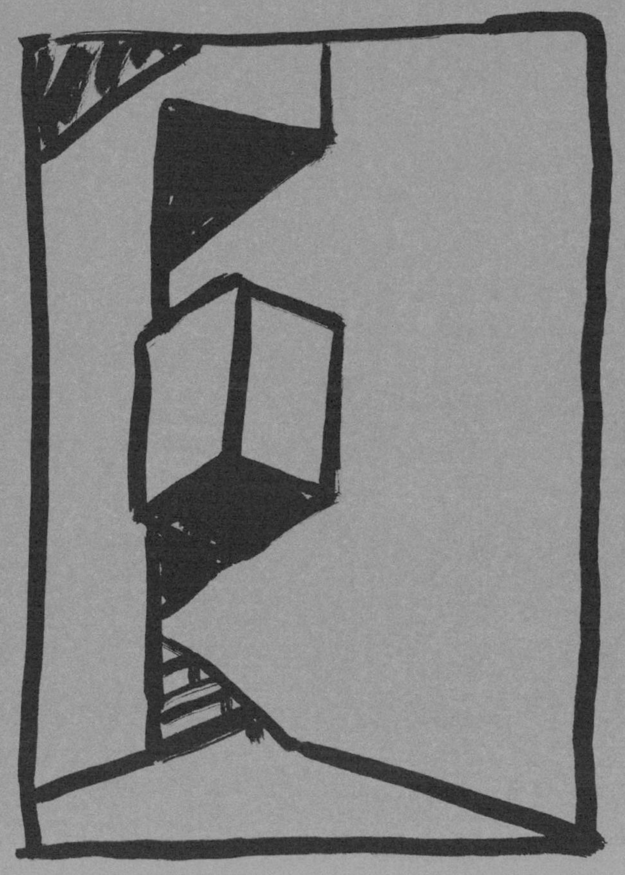

5
Lily Stockman quoted in Mara Veitch, "Lily Stockman's Love Affair with a Le Corbusier–Designed Paris Home Drives Her Latest Show," *Cultured*, May 28, 2024, https://www.culturedmag.com/article/2024/05/28/lily-stockman-le-corbusier-paris-show.

6
A widely repeated quote; see for instance https://en.wikipedia.org/wiki/Open_Hand_Monument.

7 Gavlak Gallery, "Lily Stockman—Studio Visit," undated, https://www.gavlakgallery.com/news-events/lily-stockman-studio-visit.

8 Quoted in William Middleton, "The New World of Charlotte Perriand," *Gagosian Quarterly*, Winter 2019, https://gagosian.com/quarterly/2020/02/12/essay-new-world-charlotte-perriand/.

In Stockman's homage, image becomes energy; the form alludes to a hand, surely, but also to eggs and bellies, weavings and webs. *Apollinaire*—a hypnotic composition of a black rectangle hovering above a shimmering, loose figure-eight lemon-yellow ground, framed in gradations of burnt umber and purple—is a reference to the experimental poet and art critic who coined the term "Cubism" and was so important to the development of Surrealism.

Talking to Stockman, it's clear that while art and design have certainly influenced her thinking about what art can be, so have weavings, textiles, maps, and birdsong; music, poems, flowers, the rich earth, and the infinite sky; the heat shimmer of the desert and the patterns of rain:

"My paintings are exercises in noticing, too. In good, even, natural light you'll see the layers of underpainting, and subtle chromatic harmonies—Payne's grey with a little cremnitz white and a lot of medium painted over linen gives you this earthy, subtle herbaceous color, for instance. Same as sagebrush in winter light. Each aspect of the painting shifts depending on your perspective, the light, your willingness to look a little longer."[7]

In this, her work recalls the words of the architect Charlotte Perriand, who took part in the renovation works in the gallery, in 1928. "Art," she said, "is in everything. It is in a gesture, a vase, a cooking pan, a glass, a sculpture, a piece of jewelry, a way of carrying yourself. Making love is an art."[8]

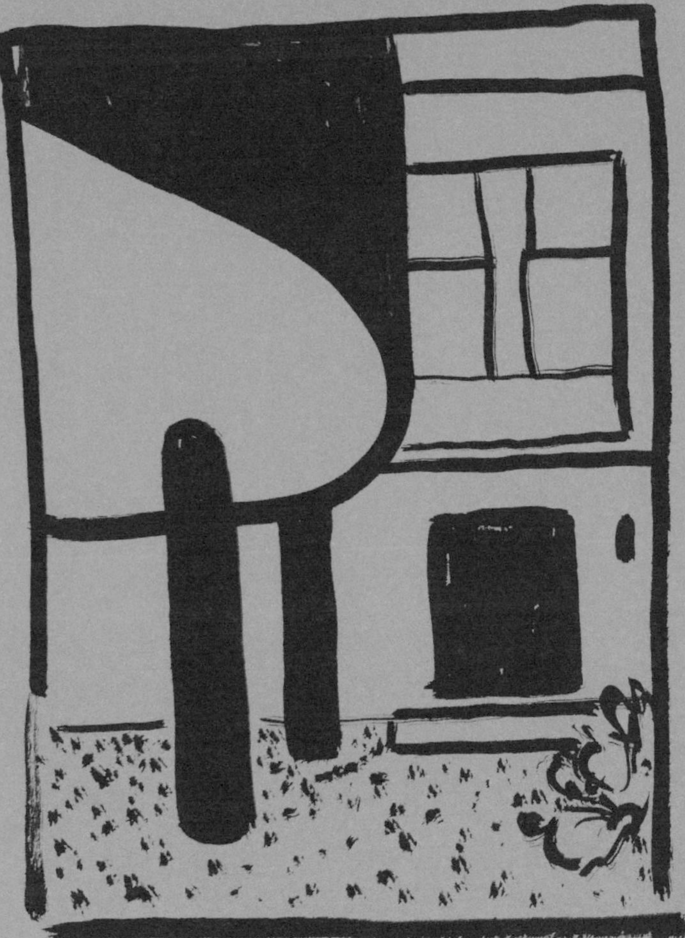

I ask Stockman how closely the shapes she employs are related to specific symbols. She replies, "I sometimes think of the central character as the noun floating among the rest of the sentence of the painting, or as the proper noun that comes from *thangka* painting." She says she has learned two main things: "To pay attention to the natural world around me, and to develop my own kind of elastic language within these very simple shapes that I have carried into a new—my own—type of language." And what does abstraction mean to her? Her reply is swift: "It's like a living thing, because it can be true without being an illustration of the truth. I think it's freedom."

LILY STOCKMAN IN CONVERSATION WITH *Nicolas Trembley*

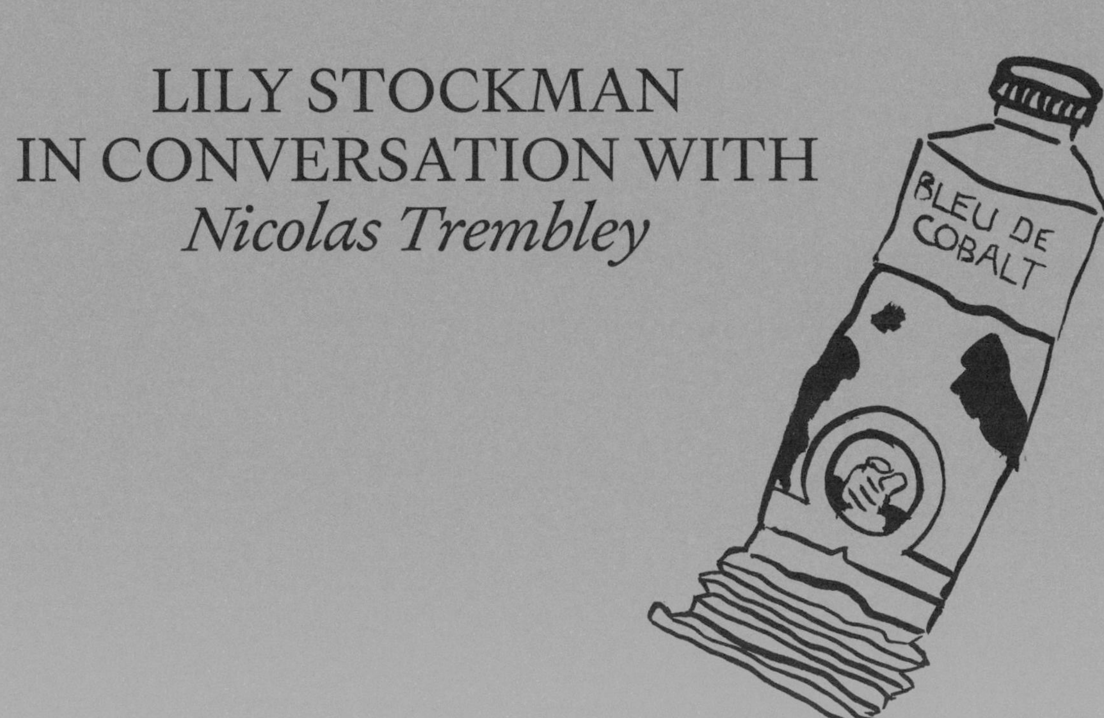

NICOLAS TREMBLEY

Lily, what's your background? Where do you come from, and how did the context you were raised in influence you?

LILY STOCKMAN

I grew up the eldest of four sisters on a farm in New Jersey. Hayfields, apple orchards, horse country. My mom made us memorize Emily Dickinson at the dinner table, and my dad made us stack hay and coached us in pond hockey, so I grew up in a kind of anachronistic world—no TV, no malls, not the '90s childhood most of my friends and classmates experienced. My world was entirely formed around nature. Calling for great horned owls and catching salamanders, building forts in the woods, knowing a wood thrush by its song, that type of thing. I'm grateful to my parents for raising us that way, because I think my sisters and I are all at home in the natural world. We are all observant and know how to look, how to see. That's good for painting.

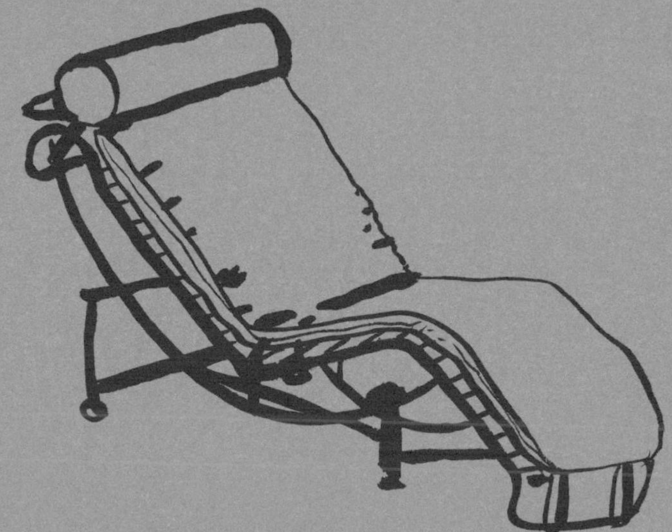

NICOLAS TREMBLEY

Tell me about your schooling. What did you study?

LILY STOCKMAN

I studied painting at Harvard. The specter of the New England historical canon—Massachusetts Bay Colony, Cotton Mather, the Concord Transcendentalists, Walden Pond, W. E. B. Du Bois, Henry James—is so deeply embedded in a Harvard education, there's no escaping its influence. Nancy Mitchnick ran the painting department like a renegade Kunsthalle, and she was enormously influential in my wanting to become a painter. She would blow the class budget every term on a massive Flemish still life with a real boar's head or lamb she would roast, heaps of tulips and overripe fruit, and we would paint it all day and then eat it at night during a huge party. During one such preparation, she admonished me for cutting up a pepper inelegantly, exclaiming, "How can you be a good painter if you can't cut a vegetable beautifully?" I still think about that every time I'm cutting peppers.

I went to NYU for my MFA, which could not have been more radically different. It was less intellectual and more of an attitude. I found it wonderful. The faculty were completely absent, there was no schedule, and the students were completely on their own to manage their time and make work. NYU's Barney Building, where the studios are, is in the heart of the East Village and still ground zero for a roving cast of downtown artists coming through and doing eight-hour-long crits, smoke breaks, and borscht at two in the morning across the street at Veselka, the beloved twenty-four-hour Ukrainian café.

Ross Bleckner, Billy Sullivan, David Salle, Tip Dunham, Lyle Ashton Harris, Ellen Berkenblit, the performance artist Claude Wampler, B. Wurtz, Dan Graham, the critic Martha Schwendener, Bob Nickas, the novelist Rick Moody, the poet Wayne Koestenbaum. Understated female powerhouses Maureen Gallace, Carol Bove, and the quicksilver Trisha Donnelly (with whom everyone fell in love) provided the spiritual center and feminine energy for our downtown world.

This was around 2011, 2012, and classmates of mine were very much concerned about the internet. Brad Troemel had just launched his influential Tumblr collaborative *The Jogging,* which quickly established a new class: net artist. My time at NYU was a quick education in the machinations of the art world and the anti-art world, which is still the art world. I loved every minute of it, although I felt completely outside and other, heading uptown to the Met to look at old stuff, not caring much about Jacques Lacan, and making oil paintings at night. But it was an inclusive group. Everyone was a freak, and it was fine that I was a painter. At Yale they would have crucified me!

NICOLAS TREMBLEY

Do you remember your first encounter with art, and how you figured out that you wanted to be an artist?

LILY STOCKMAN

I recall it quite vividly. I grew up not far from the Princeton University campus, and in the summers we would drive into town in my dad's old F150 to get ice cream and eat it while climbing the massive bronze Henry Moore sculpture, which I imagine was not permitted. It was my first memory of climbing *through* a space—from reality, the grown-up world, into an imaginary world, a child's world. I loved how the metal felt cool on my skin on a hot summer night. I liked the clangy, metallic smell of it, I loved the voluptuousness and scale. It's my first memory of really experiencing what Helen Molesworth calls the "full sensuous encounter" with a work of art.

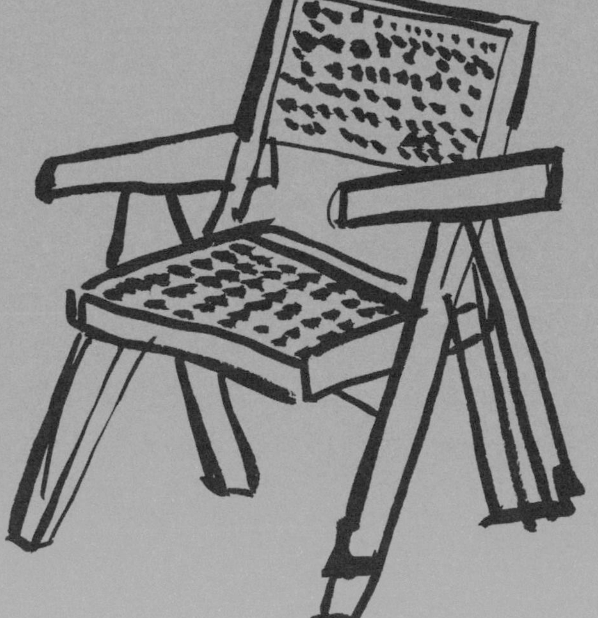

I wanted to be an artist since an early age, and I was always getting into trouble for drawing horses instead of doing multiplication tables. But I didn't really know you could actually *be* an artist until I met George Condo and the wonderful, late Stephen Mueller as visiting faculty at Harvard. They said, "Just move to New York and be an artist." Can you imagine that?! So casually? Ha! It's taken me twenty years!

NICOLAS TREMBLEY

What are you looking at, and what are your main sources of inspiration? What are the subjects that fascinate you?

LILY STOCKMAN

Art history, the natural world, Amish quilts, the patterns of mown hayfields, Shaker gift drawings, the rhyme scheme in Episcopal hymns—the language of my paintings is assembled from this very American phrase book. I love New England regionalist folk painters like Ammi Phillips, and early American modern painters like Marsden Hartley, Arthur Dove, Georgia O'Keeffe, those guys. Early Italian Renaissance painters and their architecture, like Fra Angelico, Pontormo, Giotto. The colors are so intense, more than five hundred years later, it brings a painter to tears to see them in person. The scruffy vitality and dappled light of Pierre Bonnard and Édouard Vuillard. Also just the life of Los Angeles in the very present tense—graffiti on warehouses along the LA River, run-down art deco movie palaces, freeways as outlines and borders, bougainvillea overtaking stucco buildings in shocks of pink and orange. These are all visual, aren't they?

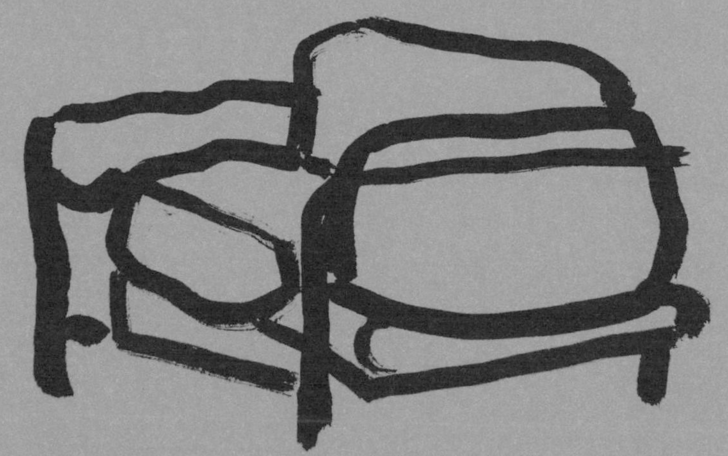

NICOLAS TREMBLEY

Yes. I understand you're interested in craft issues. Can you explain?

LILY STOCKMAN

I love thinking of them as craft "issues." I supported myself for a long time with the family textile business I started with my sister (who is also a painter). We designed block prints, working closely with a family-run block printing studio in Jaipur, where I was living at the time. Block printing is printmaking, and I think my painting process is very much like working a giant copper plate.

NICOLAS TREMBLEY

Tell me more about the process. How important is the studio for you? Do you have a daily practice? A routine? How do you organize your work?

LILY STOCKMAN

My studio is my sanctuary. Without it I would shrivel up and turn inside out like a salted slug. I have three very young children, so after I drop them off at school I am off to work, door closed, music on, by 8:30 a.m. sharp. I make an espresso and get right to it, picking up where I left off the night before.

I have a big whiteboard with my deadlines, post-it notes around the studio, a wall covered in neatly pinned source material, architectural models and stacks of books here and there, and I've kept a red Moleskine notebook since my twenties, where all my to-do lists, painting ideas, and little life notes are. Paintings large and small are hanging on the walls, and the middle of the studio is filled with works in progress lying flat on sawhorses. I work flat because I thin my oil down so much, it would drip on an upright canvas.

I work union hours: 8:30 to 5:30 Monday through Friday. At noon I break and join my studio neighbors outside—there are five of us women and a coterie of studio assistants and nine dogs altogether—and we enjoy lunch together around a big table under a giant carrotwood tree. I love painting alone all day but I *love* our chatty lunches, when we catch up on gossip and debate shows we've seen.

When I'm on deadline, I go back to work after dinner and my children go down, from eight to midnight or two in the morning. I often work on the weekends. It is completely unsustainable, and yet I work this way toward every show, to the point of collapse.

NICOLAS TREMBLEY

How do you paint? How do you start? Do you have an image in mind before?

LILY STOCKMAN

I paint flat, as I said, with the big paintings on sawhorses and the small ones on tables. I start with two colors. What is their relationship? How do they feel together? I take written notes when I'm out and about, like GOOD SUNRISE THIS MORNING / COBALT VIOLET AND ACID LEMON and then I'll make a painting starting with those written color prompts. A lot of my painting ideas come out of language, or the end of language. What is your favorite poem you turn to again and again?

The drawing happens on the painting, quick and loose. I'll start sketching with diluted oil paint and then rub it out, fine tuning it, with a rag doused in lavender spike oil, which smells incredible. The paintings are very imprecise and rough in the early stages, and then I build up the layers of color and they get more precise, more in control.

NICOLAS TREMBLEY

When do you know a piece is finished? What does "finished" mean to you?

LILY STOCKMAN

Anne Truitt wrote that she knew a painting was done when it lay down and got quiet. I love that. The past few years I think I've been hungry to push the paintings to the brink without losing the light or the ferocity of color, then rein them in just in time to keep them in control of themselves. Often the paintings go off the rails and the light goes out, so to speak—the paint gets too thick and the light can't bounce back through the layers. But sometimes there's a tension between the deliberate structure and the insouciant, unplanned mark that really makes a painting sing. Then I know it's time to stop painting.

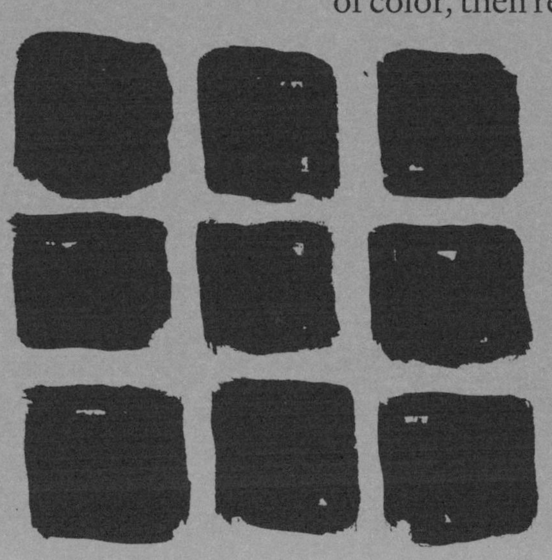

NICOLAS TREMBLEY

Are you working in series? Do you start a new painting when the last one is finished, or do you work simultaneously?

LILY STOCKMAN

I always work in series. Each show is like a research project—a historical event, a novel, a poem, a landscape I hold in my mind's eye. I've always got a few paintings cooking at once, which is more practical than conceptual because the oil paint can take so long to dry.

I've lived in Los Angeles for over a decade now, but I still make hayfield paintings from my childhood in New Jersey. All my green paintings come out of my memory or longing for New Jersey summers, the scent of freshly mown timothy.

I just did a whole series of paintings based on drawings I made at the premiere of Philip Glass's complete *Etudes*, performed at the Frank Gehry–designed Disney Concert Hall in LA. The wood paneling inside has the effect of being inside the belly of a whale, and the marks in the paintings look, to me, like the percussive notes of the piano.

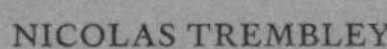

NICOLAS TREMBLEY

Do you give titles to your works? What is the inspiration for those titles?

LILY STOCKMAN

All the titles are short, always the names of places, birds, plants—references to real things to tether the paintings to the real world. Sometimes I steal a line from a poem or the title of a book.

NICOLAS TREMBLEY

How do you install your pieces in an exhibition? What is the importance of display and architecture? Can you talk about the installation in the villa?

LILY STOCKMAN

I ask myself: What is the relationship between the imagery in the paintings and the architectural vernacular of the space? How do the proportions of the paintings relate to the doorways, windows, ceiling height, and elevation changes in the room? What is the history of the building, and how do my paintings relate to or ignore that history? Maison La Roche was the most specific architecture I've worked with, and the research took over my studio: a scale model, paint samples from the rooms, archival photos from its history. The Maison became my muse, and it was thrilling to finally see the show installed in the space in person.

NICOLAS TREMBLEY

You wrote in your introduction to this book: "Le Corbusier taught me how to bring the outside inside." What does it mean?

LILY STOCKMAN

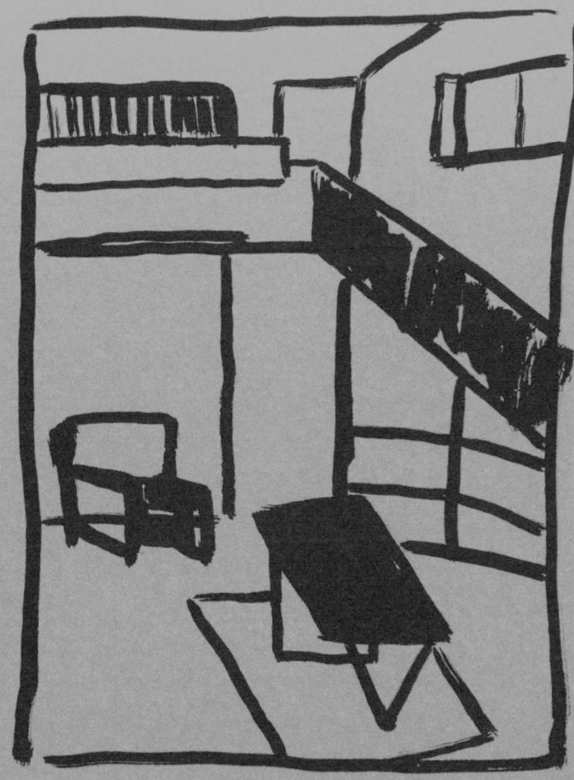

The art department where I went to college, a hulking concrete building called the Carpenter Center for the Visual Arts, was designed by Le Corbusier. It stands out starkly from the traditional Georgian brick buildings of the rest of the Harvard campus. It was designed to model the five points Corbu outlined in *Toward a New Architecture* (1923), so the painting atelier on the third floor was oriented on the north side of the building for the loveliest diffused painting light. The Carpenter was one of Corbu's last buildings, and he designed it to be a "synthesis of the arts"—the union of architecture with painting and sculpture. There is so much glass in the building that you can really see people painting and welding in the studios from the outside, especially at night. But we were also very aware of the outside world—not just the visual environment, but the intellectual and political ones, too—and absorbed it into our youthful and earnest artwork. Robert E. Fulton's *Reality's Invisible* (1971) is an incredible short 16mm film of the Carpenter Center, with scenes from student studios. You can find it online.

NICOLAS TREMBLEY

Do you feel associated with a community or a movement?

LILY STOCKMAN

I love LA. The "scene" is anti-scene; there are so many factions that overlap. My circle of friends includes photographers, landscape designers, chefs, writers, public defenders, therapists. Not just painters. I think in LA you are grappling with the pervasive anti-historicity of the tradition here; it's a lot of jump cuts, from Indigenous history to oil derricks to old Hollywood to Ed Ruscha to Catherine Opie.

I shared a warehouse with Ruby Neri along the LA River with a number of wonderful artists who all happened to be women, and the energy and camaraderie in that building was contagious. I was heartbroken to leave, but I needed more space and heat and cooling. The warehouse would get so hot, the oil would separate from my pigment, and so cold in winter, we would work in full snowsuits and fingerless gloves. Hilary Pecis found a new studio building across the river and we both moved, and now it's full of other wonderful, ambitious women who are all also working mothers. Everyone has a terrific work ethic, and we all respect and encourage each other. It's enormously powerful to have that sense of community.

NICOLAS TREMBLEY
Is there anything you would like to make people conscious of through your art?

LILY STOCKMAN
To discover they had more connection to the natural world than they supposed.

NICOLAS TREMBLEY
Thank you Lily.

LILY STOCKMAN
Thank you Nicolas, this has been a delight.

LIST OF WORKS

Dahlias of La Tour

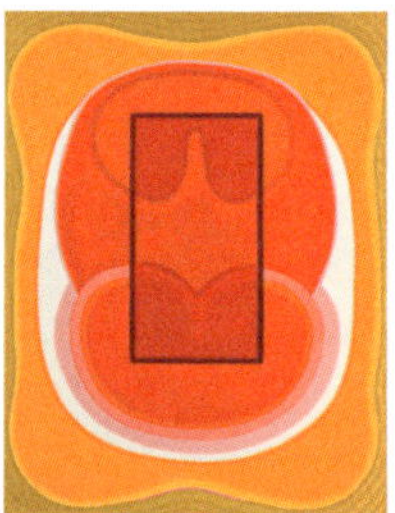

213.3 × 157.5 cm
84 × 62 inches

This work is named after a photograph Joan Mitchell took of the red and orange dahlias in her French garden, which were nodding in the breeze faster than the shutter could capture them; the photograph is blurry and makes an impression so reminiscent of a Mitchell painting. I saw this image while researching in Mitchell's archive for an essay about her late-1970s paintings. I was thinking about color, speed, light touch, and the memory of landscape.

On A Clear Day

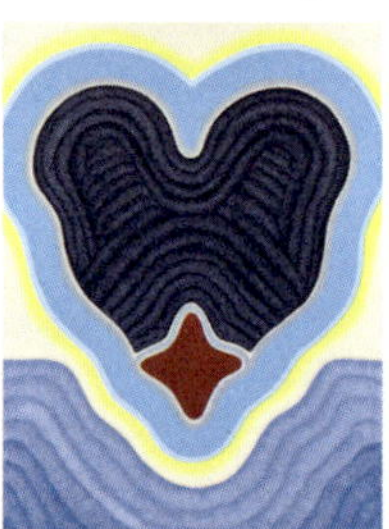

121.9 × 91.4 cm
48 × 36 inches

I made this painting specifically for the floating blue wall and thought about the reflective black square tiles on the floor. The title is a reference to an Agnes Martin suite of screen prints from 1973. It was the first time she broke the grid out of a single picture plane and separated it into multiple works to be hung together. It was also the beginning of her working serially.

Metronome

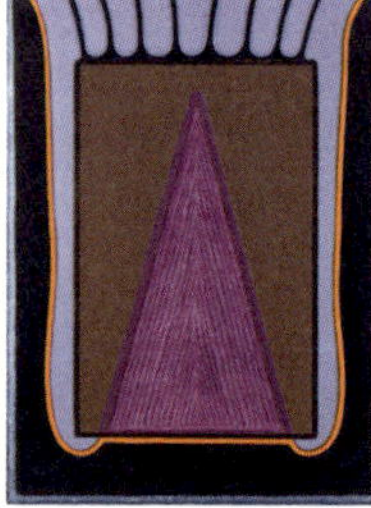

213.3 × 157.5 cm
84 × 62 inches

I read that Corbu grew up in a Swiss village known for its watchmaking, and I always thought of him as, ultimately, a keeper of time. While making this painting, I recalled the beautiful wooden metronome of my childhood music teacher—the agony of its authority and the delight of its workmanlike simplicity. The brown ramp and pale blue buttresses of the lighting system in the main room served as formal inspiration for this painting, with the natural light shifting throughout this luminous space imagined as a way of keeping time.

Chandigarh

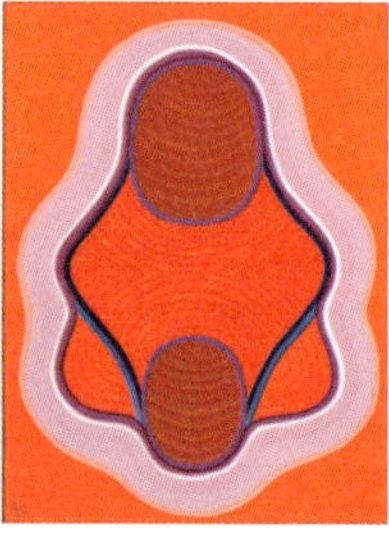

213.3 × 157.5 cm
84 × 62 inches

While living in Rajasthan a decade ago, I made a pilgrimage to Chandigarh, the capital city of Punjab, which Corbu was commissioned to design after Partition. While in Chandigarh I made another pilgrimage to see Nek Chand's fantastical folk art "city" built out of the rubble from the construction site cleared for the new capital city. At the time of my visit, Chandigarh was focused on creating the largest rose garden in South Asia, and I remember driving through acres of roses on the way to Chand's rock garden and being overwhelmed by the fragrance and the heat on the red earth. One of Corbu's letters from his time in Punjab, in 1959, reads in part: "The city of Chandigarh is planned to human scale. It puts us in touch with the infinite cosmos and nature. It provides us with places and buildings for all human activities by which the citizens can live a full and harmonious life. Here the radiance of nature and heart are within our reach." Chand's city is built just shy of human scale. The stone and glass figures are child-sized, and the parade of cement horses goat-sized. While the Capitol Complex was guarded by soldiers and barricaded by silence, Chand's world was full of families on holiday, children exploring, and people just out enjoying a respite from the city.

Sukhna Lake

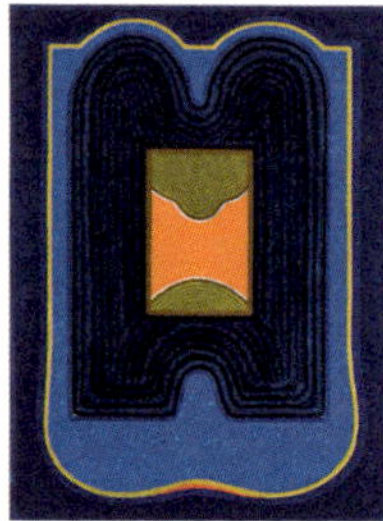

213.3 × 157.5 cm
84 × 62 inches

In Chandigarh, I had just come from the Capitol Complex, Corbu's masterpiece, and was thinking about the reflecting pools around the building, which were designed for that lofty activity, but serve, practically, as a moat to keep us non-government civilians at bay. I couldn't get inside his buildings, so abandoned my mission and killed the afternoon rowing around Sukhna Lake in the blistering midday sun. The heat was so powerful, every surface rippled in mirage, reminding me of the exquisite *phulkari* counted-thread embroideries a family friend had showed me, which she had inherited from many generations of Punjabi women in her family. The scumbled brush marks throughout my work are probably inspired by embroidery (as well as birdsong, and sound and music in general).

The Architect

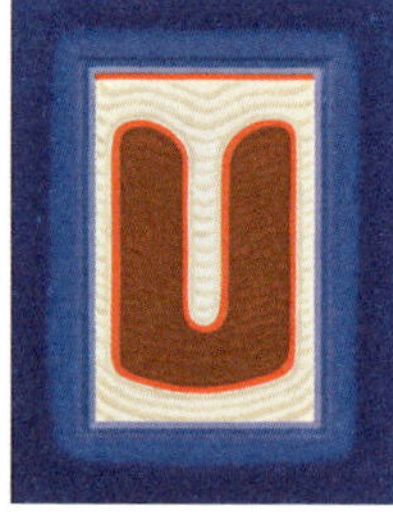

121.9 × 91.4 cm
48 × 36 inches

Perhaps the tightest painting in the bunch. I drew the head of the bull on the canvas many times in thinned-out paint, and the painting became tighter and clearer as I worked up the surface. I was looking at lots of Corbu collages, and when I made the scumbled marks on the beige ground, I was thinking of the dimpled, rumpled old paper he used. I was also thinking about Eileen Gray's small masterpiece of a house, E.1027, a modernist villa in Roquebrune-Cap-Martin, France, and the murals Corbu painted there while on holiday. I did a show on the history of the house nearly a decade ago, and it was wonderful to revisit the history through this new lens.

June Morning

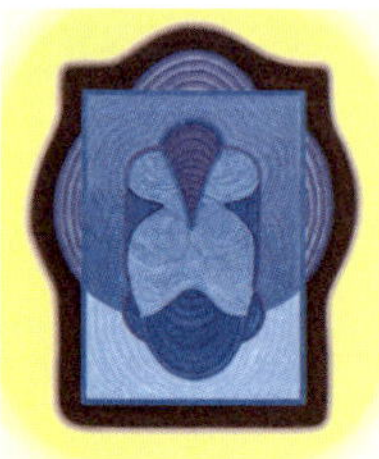

157.5 × 127 cm
62 × 50 inches

This work is about a memory of running through the woods in rural New England one June morning to swim in a pond. I make a lot of paintings about swimming in ponds, lakes, rivers, and the sea. I worked and worked on the center of this painting, and the blue paint is quite built up. The outer yellow aura and brown container, in contrast, were effortless and clean. I see the central urn shape as like wind pricking the surface of a swimming pond. I had this memory of breaking out of the beech trees, the leaves nearly yellow-green in their newness, the brown-black bark and the water of the pond the same color, and the cold rush of diving into the blackness. The sky above as I floated on my back was clear blue. It was the beginning of summer, and I was in love.

Apollinaire

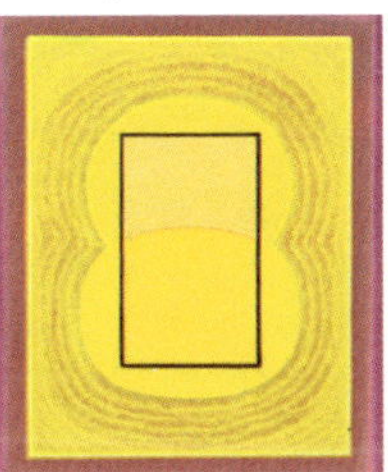

157.5 × 127 cm
62 × 50 inches

I went on a Guillaume Apollinaire tear and read about his relationship to so many conflicting movements, his charm, his championing of Cubism. Both he and Corbu were committed to creating new forms and structures in harmony with modern life. I was thinking about the rounded backs of the gunmetal-gray Thonet chairs in the dining room with those wild pink walls, and the painting mimics those shapes and colors. I also just love the idea of installing a show in a dining room, where presumably all the action happens at nighttime, in low light, and everyone's focus, their sight lines, are all inward-facing toward the table. It's the perfect place to ignore art. This painting, at night, is almost camouflaged.

Clouds Over Vétheuil

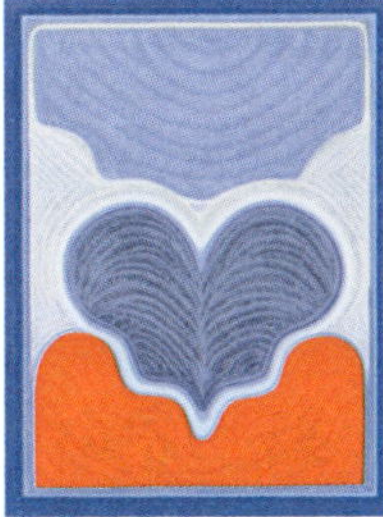

121.9 × 91.4 cm
48 × 36 inches

I thought a lot about Joan Mitchell while making this body of work, as I'd had the delight of spending quite a bit of time this past year researching her years in France for a writing project. She was so obstinate about not being influenced by Claude Monet, who had lived in Vétheuil a century before her, but of course the fact of the connection is unavoidable, and formally, from a painting perspective, thrilling. I was looking at some Monets depicting the river and the valley they both painted in, and I think the three elements of that landscape—Seine, fields, clouds—worked their way into this trisected landscape. Painting as time travel.

Black Pansy

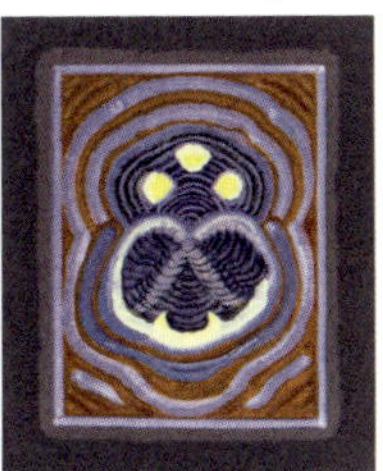

51 × 40.6 cm
20 × 16 inches

A nod to the Henri Fantin-Latour pansy paintings I love to visit at the Met. I grow pansies for their fragrance, and the big, velvety petals of the black pansy are a favorite. This painting is an outlier in the show in that it's looser and less strictly symmetrical. My friend remarked, when she saw it in my studio, "You're always painting yourself out of the paintings, but in this one, you're in it." It feels counter to Cobu's wishes to hang this, of all paintings, in the Purist room, but I actually think this is the "purest" painting in the show, because it's painted directly from life. In French art history the *pensée* means "think of me." It's like a love letter.

Blue Corydalis

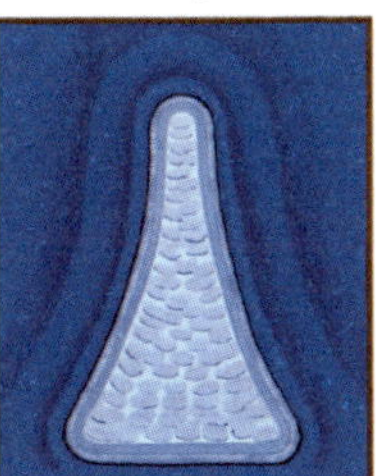

51 × 40.6 cm
20 × 16 inches

I grow porcelain-blue corydalis every spring in my modest shade garden in Los Angeles, even though it's not suited to our oppressively hot summers and invariably dies back to nubbins come August. But it thrives here in winter, giving up a profusion of the clearest blue trumpets, the hardest color to find in flowers in nature. I am always trying to grow the colors I love most in paintings. I went through a Pontormo stage where my garden was all mauves and browns and crackling oranges; now I am after Fra Angelico: jade-green hellebores, ultramarine iris, and clear blues above all, with delphinium, love-in-a-mist, and the crown prince, blue corydalis. I spent a lot of time researching Corbu's use of the color blue in his buildings, and his blue palette runs throughout my paintings in this show.

ALL WORKS
Lily Stockman, 2024
ALL IMAGES
© Ed Mumford
ALL INSTALL IMAGES
© Nicolas Brasseur,
except p. 2, 55, 81 © Aurélien Mole
Courtesy the artist,
MASSIMODECARLO,
and Fondation Le Corbusier

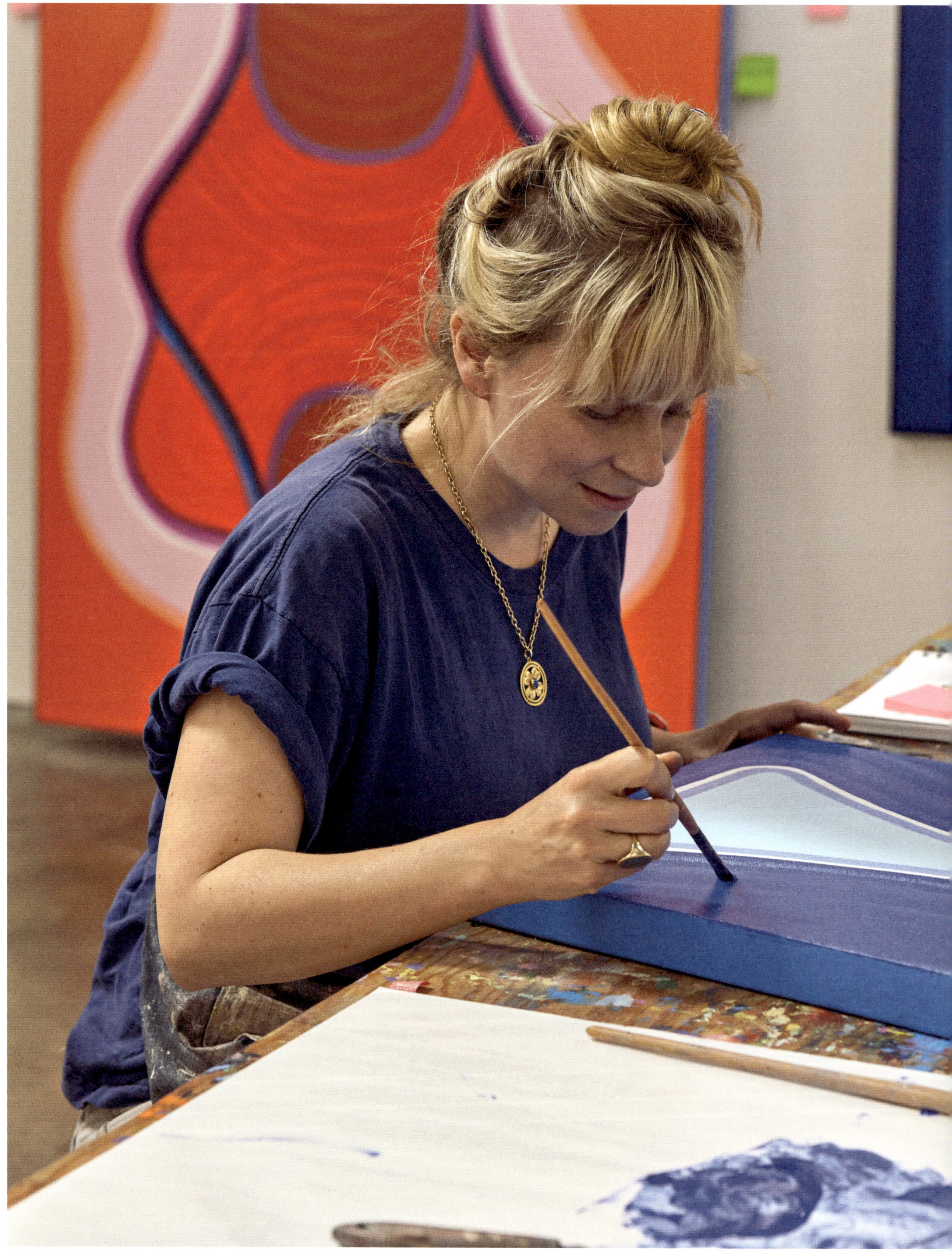

Lily Stockman

(b. 1982, Providence, Rhode Island) is a painter based in Los Angeles and Yucca Valley, California. Her paintings reflect a wide range of references and inspirations, from natural phenomena—vernal pools, mineral licks, birdsong, black ice—to historical endeavors of the spirit—Shaker gift drawings, medieval hocketing, portable Renaissance altarpieces, poetry meter. Her essays have appeared in numerous publications, most recently in *Joan Mitchell: 1979–1985* (David Zwirner, 2024). Stockman's work is in the permanent collections of the Hirshhorn Museum, Washington, DC; the Museum of Contemporary Art, Los Angeles; the Institute of Contemporary Art, Miami; the Peabody Essex Museum, Salem, Massachusetts; and the Orange County Museum of Art, Costa Mesa, California, where she was included in the 2022 California Biennial, *Pacific Gold*. Recent exhibitions explored Virginia Woolf's modern novel *The Waves* at Massimo De Carlo, London (2023); birds, plants, and weather in Emily Wilson's English translation of Homer's *Odyssey* at Gagosian, Athens (2023); and early modernist architecture at Fondation Le Corbusier, Paris (2024).

This book was published on the occasion of the exhibition *Minotaur* by Lily Stockman at Fondation Le Corbusier - Maison La Roche (May 28 – June 29, 2024). Both the exhibition and publication have been conceived and produced by MASSIMODECARLO.

Fondation Le Corbusier:

Director
Brigitte Bouvier

Head of Visitor Development, Communication and Partnerships
Gwenaelle Dubreuil

The mediation team and all other staff members

Published and distributed by
Mousse Publishing
Contrappunto s.r.l.
Via Pier Candido Decembrio 28,
20137, Milan–Italy

Available through
Mousse Publishing, Milan
moussemagazine.it

Publishing editor
Ilaria Bombelli, Mousse

Proofreading and Copyediting
Lindsey Westbrook

Book Design
Massimiliano Pace, Mousse

First edition
2025

Printed in Italy by
Grafiche Antiga spa

ISBN 978-88-6749-657-0

€ 30 / $ 35

Acknowledgements
The artist wishes to acknowledge Fondation Le Corbusier for opening the doors of Maison La Roche to this project with such generosity and enthusiasm. Thank you to Massimo De Carlo, Ludovica Barbieri, Samantha Sheiness, and their exceptional colleagues, whose passion and creativity set the high-water mark for collaboration, as well as Flavio Del Monte, Anthony Bigot and the bookmakers at Mousse. I am indebted to my college professor Nancy Mitchnick, who set me on my course as a painter and lover of Le Corbusier. And thank you to my partner in all things, Peter Brooks.

The publisher would like to thank all those who have kindly given their permission for the reproduction of material for this book. Every effort has been made to obtain permission to reproduce the images and texts in this catalogue. However, as is standard editorial policy, the publisher is at the disposal of copyright holders and undertakes to correct any omissions or errors in future editions.

All rights reserved. No part of this publication may be reproduced in any form or by any electronic means without prior written permission from the copyright holders.

© 2025 Mousse Publishing,
the artist, the authors of the texts

All works by Lily Stockman:
© Lily Stockman

All drawings by Lily Stockman
After furnitures by Pierre Jeanneret (p. 106), and Le Corbusier, Pierre Jeanneret, and Charlotte Perriand (p. 97, 99, 100, 105, 107)

All the pictures of the La Roche house by Le Corbusier and Pierre Jeanneret:
© FLC/ADAGP

All works by Le Corbusier:
© FLC by SIAE

MASSIMODECARLO

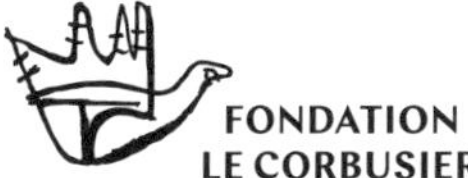